Still Preaching After All These Years...

40 *more* Seasonal Homilies

William J. Bausch

TWENTY-THIRD PUBLICATIONS
185 WILLOW STREET • PO BOX 180 • MYSTIC, CT 06355
TEL: 1-800-321-0411 • FAX: 1-800-572-0788
E-MAIL: ttpubs@aol.com • www.twentythirdpublications.com

Twenty-Third Publications
A Division of Bayard
185 Willow Street
P.O. Box 180
Mystic, CT 06355
(860) 536-2611 or (800) 321-0411
www.twentythirdpublications.com
ISBN:1-58595-327-X

Library of Congress Catalog Card Number: 2004100383
Printed in the U.S.A.

Contents

Introduction

*Now the Lord came and stood there calling as before,
"Samuel! Samuel!" And Samuel said, "Speak, Lord,
for your servant is listening."*

1 Samuel 3:10

The Lord spoke to Samuel. Samuel listened. Then Samuel in turn spoke to the people. The double rhythm of these words resonates with every preacher. He or she beseeches the Lord to speak and then listens carefully and studies and ponders the divine word. Now he or she rises up and awesomely, like Samuel, becomes the speaker, and the congregation is asked to ponder his or her words, to ponder what we have come to call the homily: the application, the translation, the reworking of the Lord's word for the contemporary audience.

No small challenge, no small burden. But we do what we can, however imperfectly. Therefore, these forty homilies are hardly the standard. They are but one preacher's limited attempt and are to be taken as circumscribed by all the natural restrictions that make up anyone's time and place in history and in society. To this extent they beg to be digested and translated by another's talent. Even those homilies the reader might consider lesser ones can be mined for further thoughts and exposition. In any case, if these homilies provide that much fodder, then I shall consider my attempt worthwhile. The Lord has spoken. We have listened. Now it's our turn to speak in the Lord's name.

A note: To maintain the freshness of the homilies, I have kept

1

national, regional, and local references. So, for example, if the Quecreek miners' drama in chapter 8, the references to Joe Millionaire, Jennifer Lopez, and Eminem in chapter 9 or the statistics for my New Jersey municipalities on alcohol and drugs in chapter 11 do not resonate or apply any longer, just use your common sense and replace them with other current examples. There will be, alas, at any time, no lack of them at hand.

I have noticed in hindsight that collectively these homilies seem frequently to center around two major themes: the persistent presence of Jesus in our lives and the persistent call to genuine discipleship. Not bad themes for troubled times.

Advent & Christmas

Christ the Ever-Green

Mark 13:33–37

All of us can readily sense the different tone as we meet today. The banner is different. The flowers are gone. The bright green of the vestments have given way to somber purple. The Advent wreath is present, soon to be lit. All is different from last week. We, as a Catholic people, know that we have left an old Church year and today begin a new one with this holy season of Advent.

Like the start of the secular new year, the beginning of a new Christian year and the end of an old one prompt us to look at two questions. The first question is this: in the past liturgical year how has God touched me in my most happy times? Think of good fortune, friendships, health, the things that went well, the things that made you happy. Did you recognize God's presence in them? If not specifically then, it's easy to do so now, in hindsight.

The second question is harder: how has God touched me in my most painful times? The hurts, the breakups, the ill health, the betrayals, the disappointments, the deaths, the losses, the tears? Did I recognize God's presence there? If not specifically then, it's still hard to do now, in hindsight. Yet God was there, too.

One man's story might offer a hint of how God is present in the painful times. Henry Viscardi was born with stumps instead of fully developed legs. He learned to walk well on his stumps and was capable of living a normal life, but the prejudices of others hurt him very much. When Henry was reduced to crying out, "Why me?" his mother would tell him, "When it was time for another crippled boy to be born, the Lord and his council held a meeting to decide where he should be sent, and the Lord said, 'I think the Viscardis would be a good family to take care of him.'" It was just a simple story, but it made Henry feel like he had a place and a purpose in life. He stopped asking "Why me?" and began making the most of his abilities.

Henry did very well in school, and he eventually graduated from Fordham University. After years of trying to walk like a normal person, Henry had damaged the skin and tissue of his stumps. He knew that without prosthetic legs, he would have to use a wheelchair. But no prosthetic could be found to fit him. Doctor after doctor said it was hopeless.

But then one day a German doctor committed himself to inventing a prosthesis that would work for Henry. It took a few months, but the doctor finally created a workable pair of legs. For the first time in his life, Henry Viscardi looked and walked like a normal man. When he tried to pay for the legs, the doctor refused to accept it. Here is what he said to Henry, "There's no bill now. But someday, if you'll make the difference for one other individual—the difference between a life dependent on charity and one rich with dignity and self-sufficiency—our account will be square."

Henry joined the Red Cross during World War II, and he dedicated himself to helping new amputees deal with their situation. When the war ended, Henry witnessed the problems that many disabled veterans had in getting jobs. So he gathered together a group of sympathetic business leaders and created Just One Break, or JOB, an organization that finds jobs for people with disabilities.

Next, Henry started Abilities, Inc., with the same goal in mind. That was over forty years ago. Today, Abilities, Inc. has grown into the National Center for Disabilities Services, which runs a school for children with disabilities. All of their efforts are aimed at educating, empowering, and rehabilitating those with physical disabilities. Henry says today, "I can't help but believe that the Lord had a plan for my life that made me the way I was and let me become who I am."

I want Henry's story to tell you forcefully that God was there in the painful times of last year, helping you become who you are today. I want to remind you again that God's presence is never absent, although, as we said, it is harder to detect in our sorrowful times. Yet sometimes we need a reminder, a sign, a symbol of that presence. So in closing, I want to offer you a sign that is common to our area, especially now when winter is starting to be felt and the landscape will soon be covered with snow. An old Cherokee story provides it. It goes like this:

When the world was first created, the Great Mystery gave a gift to each species. But first he set up a contest to determine which gift would be most useful to whom. "You will be the guardians of the forest," he said to the trees and the plants. "Even in the seeming dead of winter your brother and sister creatures will find life protected in your branches.

"I want you to stay awake and keep watch over the earth for seven nights," he told them. The young trees and plants were so excited to be entrusted with such an important job that the first night they did not find it difficult to stay awake. The second night was not so easy, however, and just before dawn a few fell asleep. On the third night the trees and plants whispered among themselves in the wind, trying to keep from dropping off to sleep, but it was too much work for some of them. Even more fell asleep on the fourth night.

By the time the seventh night came, the only trees and plants still awake were the cedar, the pine, the spruce, the fir, the holly, and the laurel. "What wonderful endurance you have," exclaimed the Great Mystery. "You shall be given the gift of remaining green forever." Ever since then, all the other trees and plants lose their leaves and sleep all winter while the evergreens, ever alert, give color to the bleak landscape.

This story says a great deal. It preaches that out there somewhere, in the winter times of our lives as in the winter of Henry Viscardi's life, is Christ the Ever-green. The evergreen is a symbol, a sign, which says that even in our worst times, God's love abides and remains firm. In our most sinful times, God's love, as it were, remains green. We cannot shake his leaves nor brown him out.

Once again, it's Advent. The skies are gray, the ground is getting hard, and the trees are barren. It's cold outside. The color is gone, except for the evergreens. It's cold inside: our soldiers are in another land waging war; at home, terrorism stalks us; families fracture, drugs kill, sex is degraded. Scandal tarnishes the Church; greed, the corporation; and exploitation, the children. The moral color is gone—except for Christ, the Ever-green.

So it's Advent again, the beginning of a new Christian year. In the midst of the good and bad of the past year, God has touched you and is about to do so again. Therefore, as we light the candle of the Advent wreath with great hope, remember that its leaves are a promise of God's abiding presence for this coming year. Note it, recognize it, and cherish it, for it is Christ, the Ever-green.

Waiters

Matthew 3:1–12

"Prepare the way of the Lord, make straight his paths."

There are all kinds of waiters. I don't mean the folks who serve your table at restaurants, but people who wait. Period. They fall into several distinctive categories and styles; you and I may find ourselves here.

There are those who remain patient and calm no matter what the circumstance, but they are rare. Far more common are the impatient ones who pace and foot tap and steal glances at their watches; who, when you finally arrive, let you know exactly how late you are; who maddeningly weave in and out of parkway traffic trying to get one car ahead of the others; who jockey to get into the express lane at the supermarket with their carriage far over the twelve-item limit; who, like the Mad Hatter, are always in a hurry.

There are the providers who bring something to read while they wait. Next there are the multi-taskers with their ubiquitous cell phones and palm pilots who can't abide the solitude and silence so necessary for emotional and spiritual growth.

Then there are those who practice a Zen-like calm, whose motto is, "when I arrive, I arrive." Their opposite are the over-anxious, who spend their time letting their imaginations run wild, sure that something terrible and disastrous has happened: the friend they are waiting for has been kidnapped or has fallen through an open manhole or was abducted by aliens. There are those who simply can't wait at all, like the children who ask "are we there yet?" or "when is Santa coming?"

There are those, too, for whom waiting is sublime, like a woman awaiting the birth of a child who is taken in by the whole experience. And there are those waiting for death, which, for some reason, stubbornly refuses to come.

Finally, there are the spiritual waiters. They have doubts to be calmed, a loneliness to be filled, a family matter to be repaired, a relationship in need of mending, a hurt that won't go away, a sickness that lingers; or they are simply waiting for some sign of God in their lives, some sign of his care, his genuine concern, his presence, his nearness, his promise, his love. If only God would whisper, "I am here." Then they could put up with anything, could wait forever.

But I think there is one common category of waiters that fits us all. Whether we ever say it out loud or not, we are the "cocooners." That is, we are all wrapped in the confining mesh of our own desires and self-centeredness and self-importance; but we know, really know, that someday, like Mary, we must let a different life take place within us. We must respond to Another. We must break free and become the profound creature we have been called to be and are, in fact, destined to be.

I am talking here about holiness. I am talking about the yearning, the desire, the longing, the waiting, the deep-down imperative that we all feel but frequently duck: the truth that we all have been called to be saints, and we wait uneasily until that is both recognized and achieved.

Graham Greene's protagonist in *The Power and the Glory* is our model for this. This hero, or non-hero really, is a seedy, alcoholic Catholic priest who, after months as a fugitive, is finally caught by the revolutionary Mexican government and condemned to be shot. On the evening before his execution, the priest sits in his cell with a flask of brandy to keep his courage up, and he thinks back over what seems to him the dingy failure of his life. Greene writes:

Tears poured down his face. He was not at that moment afraid of damnation—even the fear of pain was in the background. He felt only an immense disappointment because he had to go to God empty-handed, with nothing done at all. It seemed to him at that moment that it would have been quite easy to have been a saint. It could only have needed a little self-restraint, and a little courage. He felt like someone who had missed happiness by seconds at the appointed place. He knew now that, at the end, there was only one thing that counted—to be a saint.

To be a saint. I suggest that to learn how, we walk and talk with Mary during these Advent days. She is a woman who knew how to become a saint. She waited and waited for nine months for the quiet life within her to become the Savior, the long-desired Christ. She savored the moments of quiet and solitude for she knew they were necessary for growth, for Jesus, for holiness, for the stuff of saintliness. Her way of preparing for the birth of Jesus was far different from our hectic, pre-Christmas preparations, filled with the incessant hawking of goods, endless commercials, and jingle-bell noise. To put it mildly, these are not friendly to the interior life. This is not the climate in which to discover our destiny to be saints.

The other day I came across a little Advent prayer of confession that might urge us to some quiet, reflective time. It goes like this:

If we have spent so much time shopping that we have little time to spend with those for whom we are shopping, Lord, forgive us and give us sensitivity.

If we get so busy practicing for the Christmas programs that we forget to think about what they mean, God, forgive us and give us understanding.

If we decorate our houses but neglect the inner beauty of our homes, O God, forgive us and grant us love.

If we are worried about how much Christmas is going to cost us but have given little thought to how much

Christmas cost God, oh Lord, forgive us and give us perspective.

If we are so consumed with thinking about this Christmas that we have little consideration for the meaning of the first Christmas, oh Lord, forgive us and give us insight.

If we are overextended and bogged down with tiredness and long to see your face but cannot find it, Lord, give us a sign of hope.

If we are too much in a hurry to realize our potential, our destiny, that we are saints in-the-making, O Lord, slow us down and give us quiet and solitude.

Mary of Advent, help us prepare for the coming of the Lord.

Cause for Rejoicing

Isaiah 61:1–2, 10–11

The Spirit of the Lord God is upon me
Because the Lord has anointed me;
He has sent me to bring glad tidings to the poor,
To heal the brokenhearted,
To proclaim liberty to the captives,
To announce a year of favor
From the Lord.

How those words of Isaiah in the first reading sting! Although addressed to all of God's people, these words traditionally carry a special meaning for priests. In a special way, they are the priest's clarion call, his job description. He has been anointed to bear glad tidings, to heal, proclaim release, to announce. Yet, in the light of the ongoing and continuing revelations about sexual abuse by priests in Boston and elsewhere—some of them truly despicable—those words today seem a mockery.

But, my people, this is the Sunday of the Pink Candle. This is Rejoice Sunday and St. Paul has reminded us, "Do not quench the Spirit." And here is where I come in: to unquench that Spirit by moving you beyond the spectacle of unworthy priests to consider this morning some worthy ones.

My first example is about the very first black parish in Alexandria, Virginia, a parish now filled with every shade of skin color. The priests who built the parish are described by a woman who was there at the beginning, one of the pioneers who built the church with their dimes and dollars, saying, "These priests have always lived poor themselves. Wonderful workers." But one priest in particular stood out:

> Fr. Kanda's shoes were always falling apart. He never had any food in the house. He'd knock on the door sometimes eleven o'clock at night, bless us all, and my mother and father would bring out something for him to eat. He was young and a very, very busy person. He visited every black family in the community. The children loved him.

Any of you remember a good and loving parish priest like Fr. Kanda? There were—are—lots of them. Have they been in the news lately? Hardly.

The second example is a Colombian priest who lived and died in that violent land where the drug war continues, largely due to the addiction of five million Americans to cocaine. This was the manner of his final days of life as reported in the British publication, the *Tablet*:

> Twenty days after the killing of Archbishop Duarte of Cali, two gunmen burst into the crowded parish church of La Argentina last Saturday evening. They shot Fr. Juan Ramon Nuñez four times while he was at the altar distributing the Eucharist. Fr. Nuñez was rushed to the hospital but pronounced dead shortly after his arrival. One of his parishioners was also killed in the attack. The bishop said, "How is it possible that in the atmosphere of Christmas when we are celebrating the birth of Jesus Christ, someone, somewhere, decided to order the death of a priest who was distributing the bread of life to his community? How have we managed to distance ourselves so much from God?"

The *Tablet*, by the way, remarks, "Fr. Nuñez is the twenty-fourth priest to be killed in Colombia since 1998."

We can't even imagine living like that, yet it goes on every day in other parts of the world. Think of twenty-four priests in our own diocese gunned down because they were an affront to drug lords or evil people. The imprisonment and killing of these faithful priests goes on all the time throughout the world, but it's not the stuff of scandal. It is not camera worthy.

Then there is the recently deceased Cardinal Francis X. Van Thuan who in his book, *Testimony of Hope*, tells of his years in a Vietnamese prison. His suffering was enormous. This "Prince of the Church" spent thirteen years in prison, nine of which were in solitary confinement in a windowless room where light burned for days, followed by long periods of total darkness. He spoke of the hope he gained from meditating on the sufferings of Christ, and he spoke of his deep prayer life. He wrote down 300 Scripture quotations from memory; these words fed him during his long years of torture. He clung to the hope of Christ, and his spirit was not quenched. Yet the story of Cardinal Francis X. Van Thuan did not make the Boston *Globe*.

Finally, consider this story of a young priest whose early years were filled with death and sorrow. His mother died in his childhood; his father and elder brother, in his youth. Later on he wrote, "At twenty I had already lost all the people I loved, and even those I might have loved, like my older sister who, they said, died six years before I was born." Despite all this, and amid great turmoil in his country, he eventually became a priest and served well enough to be called in by his superior and told that his appointment as a new bishop was pending.

And listen to this, and I quote:

> Half an hour after this conversation he arrived at the convent of the Grey Ursuline sisters. He asked the nun who opened the door where the chapel was and entered it without saying another word. He strode quickly toward the altar and sank to his knees in the front pew....When the nuns went to bed, he was still in the chapel. He continued praying for eight hours.

The priest's name is Karol Wojtyla, and we know him, of course, as Pope John Paul II. This account of his earlier years does not come from biographers who are determined to say only good things about a hero. It is from Carl Bernstein, one of the famous pair who exposed the Watergate crime.

So, there we are: the poor priest in Virginia, the slain priest in Colombia, the imprisoned "Prince of the Church" in Vietnam, the scarred priest in Poland: not really material for *Larry King Live* or *20/20*. But priests such as these are legion, often at great peril to their own lives. All over the globe they bring glad tidings, heal the brokenhearted, and talk about liberty and release for those who are physically and morally imprisoned.

I guess what I am saying is that I want you to remember: that for every Fr. Shanley, there is a Fr. Kanda. For every Fr. Goeghan, there is a Fr. Nuñez. For every Cardinal Law, there is a Cardinal Van Thuan. And I would say that, for every greedy CEO, for every crooked politician, for every unscrupulous lawyer, for every unethical doctor who makes the headlines and quenches the Spirit, there are their countless decent counterparts who do not. For them—and for us—I repeat St. Paul's words: "Brothers and sisters, rejoice."

A New Year's Parable

Luke 2:16–21

On the first day God created the cow. God said, "You must go to the field with the farmer all day long and suffer under the sun, have calves, and give milk to support the farmer, and I will give you a life span of sixty years."

The cow said, "That's a kind of a tough life you want me to live for sixty years. Let me have twenty years, and I'll give back the other forty." And God agreed.

On the second day God created the dog. God said, "Sit all day by the door of your house and bark at anyone who comes in or walks past. I will give you a life span of twenty years." The dog said, "That's too long to be barking. Give me ten years, and I'll give back the other ten." So God, with a sigh, agreed.

On the third day God created the monkey. God said, "Entertain people, do monkey tricks, make them laugh. I'll give you a twenty-year life span." Monkey said, "How boring; monkey tricks for twenty years? I don't think so. Dog gave you back ten, so that's what I'll do, too, okay?" And God agreed again.

On the fourth day God created man. God said, "Eat, sleep, play, and enjoy life. Do nothing, just enjoy. I'll give you twenty years." Man said, "What? Only twenty years? No way, man. Tell you what, I'll take my twenty, and the forty cow gave back, and the ten dog gave back, and the ten monkey gave back. That makes eighty, okay?" "Okay," said God. "You've got a deal."

So that's why for the first twenty years we eat, sleep, play, enjoy life, and do nothing; for the next forty years we slave in the sun to support our family; for the next ten years we do monkey tricks to entertain our grandchildren; and for the last ten years we sit in front of the house and bark at everybody!

Where does time go? Here we are at the start of another year that inevitably transitions us from one time frame to another. I don't know if the parable holds true—although it has a certain identifiable ring to it—or where each of us is in the cow-dog-monkey stages. But I do know that time is a gift and that a new year is always a new beginning, and that, since grace abounds, spiritual opportunity will always be around the next calendar corner. To put it another way, this new year we will be invited to another stage of our lives, to a more profound involvement with the Spirit, to a deeper degree of conversion, to a challenge of being holier at the end of this new year than we have been at the end of the previous year.

And that challenge becomes increasingly more urgent as we limp into this new year. At this point in time, North Korea is revving up its nuclear capacities, Israelis and Palestinians continue to brutally kill one another, militant Muslim fanatics assassinate Christians, our country is at war, there is talk of reinstating the draft, the gap between the very rich and the very poor grows everyday wider, our Church is seriously wounded. These need not be forthcoming days of despair, however; rather, they are days of opportunity to become more virtuous, more caring, more compassionate, more Christ-like, more faithful to a gospel which has the power to reverse all these evils.

All told, we have been given, on the average, some 25,000 days to live. Some portion of that has already run out. But a New Year, remember, wipes out all of the yesterdays and offers us 365 shining, new tomorrows in which to be finer, more focused, more faithful Christians.

Of course, like last year, it's only an offer. To accept it has to be one of our most meaningful and profound New Year's resolutions.

We Are the Magi

Matthew 2:1–12

We three kings of Orient are,
Bearing gifts we traverse afar....

O, star of wonder, star of night,
Star with royal beauty bright,
Westward leading, still proceeding,
Guide us to thy perfect light.

Picturesque, delightful, magical: such is this feast of the Epiphany.

I suspect that, next to the manger scene, nothing has caught the Christian imagination more than the Magi story. It's not just that they are so colorful that each succeeding generation has had to add more and more hues; it's not just that they are so mysterious that we simply had to give them gorgeous names; it's not just that they are so wonderfully exotic that we had to count their number as a mystical three; it's not just that, since they come from a faraway land, we had to make them—what else!—kings. It's not just all of these things that have captivated us. Rather, deep down, whether we realize it or not, we instinctively know that the Magi story is our story, and that's why we are mesmerized by it. The Magi, basically, are you and I and everyone born into this world. Their timeless tale follows the human storylines of everyone.

Consider. First, for every human being, from the very moment of birth, there is a call to answer, a vision to follow, a goal to be reached, an ideal to be fulfilled. In a very real sense, we are all born with a vocation. It may be to become a mechanic, an engineer, a teacher, a dancer, whatever. The goal may be to find one's true love, the jewel in the eye of the idol, the Emerald City for Dorothy Gale, the Holy Grail for Indiana Jones, the sorcerer's stone for Harry Potter, the King of the Jews for the three searchers. We all are born with a goal to be reached. To put it another way, beneath all these symbols, there is, simply put, the human ache for God. We share this with the Magi.

Second, the Magi, in order to seek their goal, must embark on a journey and take on the risks of doing so. Sooner or later, we modern Magi also have to leave the security of what we know to venture out into the unknown.

Like it or not, from birth to death life is one inexorable journey with very discernible and identifiable stages, from infancy to adolescence to adulthood. Each stage has its set of risks. Shall the child cling to the comfort and security of the mother or take on the risks of the neighborhood and school? Can the adolescent leave his or her self-absorption and run the risk of trusting others? Can the adult pull back from an all-absorbing money-making career and take the time to foster fidelity and intimacy with another? There are risks all up and down the line.

Third, on a journey, any journey, there are always obstacles. For the Magi, there was Herod, a wicked king who sweet-talked a lie to them: "Please, go find this adorable child you are seeking and by all means come back and tell me. There is nothing more I want that to fall at those infant feet and adore him." And Herod, dreaming of murder, wiped away a sentimental tear.

For us, the obstacles to our true goal are the sweet-talking lies of commercials that try to convince us we are what we purchase and what we purchase makes us what we are; it's the rationalistic hucksters in our universities or on our TVs who preach that we have no goal, that all is here and now. There is no journey. All is illusion. There's only a straight line to oblivion, so make the most of it.

Other obstacles are the stimulating highs of drugs; the idolatry of celebrity; the lure of exciting, uncommitted sex; and the constant din provided by the ubiquitous noisemakers—their loud music and machines, their constant hectoring to buy, their heady success in teaching us to equate busyness with importance. "You must be terribly busy" has become a sort of compliment, a hint that we are important and indispensable. "Always on the go" and "There's never enough time" are badges we wearily but proudly wear. The noisemakers smile. In no way do they want us to flirt with silence and solitude, wherein we might discover our true selves and sense the real goal of our journey. Such obstacles are, if you will, the spiritual steroids that puff-up our self-importance, inflate our desire for power, and make us blind to the cry of the poor.

But there are helps, too. For the Magi, help came in the form of an angel who warned them not to return to oily Herod but to take another path. For us, there are our moral heroes and models—hopefully, beginning with our parents—who have taught us by word and example to take another path, the path of Jesus, and who have taught us who we really are: God-imaged folk made to know, love, and serve God in this life and be happy with God forever in heaven. In the best scenario, our parents are mightily aided by a faith community, the inspiration of the saints, common and faithful worship, prayer, and the sacraments.

Finally, of course, there is the end of the journey. For the Magi it was to engage the sacred, to look into the face of Christ and, falling down, to offer him their gifts and worship him. It is the same for us: to offer our gifts and talents and to minister to Jesus—which, in fact, we do whenever we feed the hungry, give drink to the thirsty, and clothe the freezing because when we do these things for the very least of humanity, we are doing them for Jesus himself.

So there we are:

Beginning, middle, end.
Birth, growth, death.
Risk, obstacles, help.
The face of God.

It's all there in today's gospel.

That's why the story of the Magi resonates so well with us. Deep in our subconscious, you see, we recognize ourselves; we are the Magi still en route. That recognition forces us to examine where we are right now on our spiritual journey, what risks we have taken for the sake of the kingdom of God, or even, perhaps, how our quest for God has been replaced by false idols or sidetracked by modern-day Herods. We are made to pause in our life journey, face up to our Herods and ask: is it possible that have we gained the whole world at the expense of our own souls? If so, we pray:

O star of wonder, star of night
Star with royal beauty bright,
Westward leading, still proceeding,
Guide us to thy perfect light.

Let Your Light Shine

Matthew 2:1–12

On this feast of the Epiphany with its theme of light, the focus is on the Magi, those mysterious figures whom tradition has given the wonderfully inventive names of Caspar, Balthazar, and Melchior, declared their number to be three, designated them as men of different races to represent all humanity coming to the Lord and even assigned exotic meanings to their gifts: gold for the sovereignty of Christ, incense for his divinity, and myrrh to foreshadow his suffering.

Of course, there is no way to disentangle all the legends and stories that have appeared throughout the ages about these mysterious folk who appear in Matthew's exotic account. But through them all we should not, must not, miss the essential reason why Matthew introduced these figures. In effect, Matthew is saying that the Magi were the first Christophers. That is, having been guided by the light of the star and having encountered the Light of the World at Bethlehem, they were now commissioned to carry that light, be that light, for others.

The Wise Men are presented to us as examples of living witnesses to the faith. They came out of the darkness to follow the light of the star to the Light of the World; then, they were to go back to let their light shine for others. "Let your light shine" could well be their motto.

That's the meaning of this feast of the Epiphany: all who have encountered God must let their light shine. So let me bring you up to date and point to how it's done in our times. Let me introduce to you two modern wise men, separated by 2000 years from the Magi but very much a part of them. As it happens, they come from the world of sports, and their stories were told in the *Wall Street Journal* under the significant title, "You Can't Be a Beacon if Your Life Don't Shine."

Over thirty-five years ago, Sandy Koufax, a Jew who was a pitcher for the Los Angeles Dodgers, announced that he would not pitch on Yom Kippur, the holiest day of the Jewish year—even though this game was the first game of the 1965 World Series. The management was aghast. They coaxed him, pleaded with him, told him to pitch just a few of his fabulous pitches and then he could go to all the synagogues in Los Angles to his heart's content. Koufax refused. It was the Sabbath day, and his religion came first. So Don Drysdale took his place and lost the game. Koufax pitched the second game and lost. But, as you may remember, the Dodgers won the 1965 series 4–3. And Koufax pitched a shutout in games five and seven. But talk about being a Magi, of letting your light shine! To pass up starting a World Series game for a matter of faith? Would you and I do that?

To come closer to our own time, there is Eli Herring, the 340-pound offense tackle for Brigham Young University. He graduated with a 3.5 grade point average and was judged to be the best offensive tackle in the draft. He is also a Mormon—a practicing one. An Epiphany man, if you will. As such, he turned down a multimillion-dollar deal with the Oakland Raiders because he won't play football on Sunday, a holy day—the day the Raiders always play. He also told the NFL that if he were drafted, he would not serve. Since he was the No. 3-ranked senior tackle in the country, he would have gone early, but he turned down the offers. He could have signed up with the NFL, played ball on Sunday, and filled his lifestyle with Rolls Royces, suburban mansions, and Brooks Brothers suits—or he could teach math for $25,000 a year and honor the Sabbath.

And, in fact, he now teaches math for $25,000 a year, instead of the $25,000,000 he could make. He coaches football at the high school level and wears chino pants and a nice Wal-Mart shirt. Talk about letting your light shine! It makes you think: ought we extend the list of wise folk? You know, Caspar, Melchior, Balthazar, Sandy, and Eli? It makes you ask the big question, consider the big challenge: could *our* names be added to that list?

The interesting thing is that, when they and we give such witness, shed such light, it has a ripple effect. Here is what Matt Weinstein wrote in his book, *Managing to Have Fun*. He said that one day he was running through the streets of Berkeley with his friend, Dale Larsen. Dale is a clinical psychologist, and although they had been friends for a long time, they had never gone running together before. After stretching, they began to run and had only gone a few blocks when Matt noticed Dale reach into the pocket of his shorts, take out a handful of coins, and throw them over his shoulder.

The first couple of times this happened, Matt pretended not to notice. But after a while it began to drive him crazy, so he finally asked, "Dale, what's the story with the money? Why are you throwing coins into the street?" Dale laughed and proceeded to tell him about an amazing psychology experiment nicknamed, interestingly enough, the Good Samaritan Study:

In the study, researchers positioned themselves across from a pay phone and studied the people who made phone calls. One of the first things they discovered was that almost everyone who makes a call looks in the coin return after hanging up to see if any coins happen to be there. The urge is irresistible: you just have to look in the coin return to see if the machine has mistakenly returned your money! This behavior gave the researchers an idea. The next day they randomly put coins in the coin return slot so that some of the people who used the phone actually did discover money.

The researchers then hired a young woman, with an arm full of books, to walk by the phone at the exact moment that the subjects were hanging it up. As the young woman walked by with her arms full of books, she pretended to stumble and drop them on the ground. Astonishingly, the researchers observed that the people who found money in the coin return were four times as likely to stop and help the woman pick up her books than were the people who found no money in the coin return. They concluded that when we feel good, we tend to do good, which also means that the helping impulse is transferable. In other words, if you do something good for another person, he or she is much more likely to do something nice for someone else, causing one small gesture to result in a giant ripple effect.

All these examples catch the spirit of the story of the Magi as Christ-bearers and Light-givers. They sought the Light, found the Light, and shared the Light. Such is the story of Epiphany— and its challenge.

Baptism: The Expectant Sacrament

Mark 1:7–11

We do it so casually that we don't even realize we're doing it. As we come into church, we dip our fingers in the holy water font and bless ourselves. Some may even say the words "In the name of the Father and of the Son and of the Holy Spirit"; but most don't. They may be still talking to their neighbors or looking around; they automatically do the gesture.

Some parishes begin Mass with a sprinkling rite, especially during the Easter season. And the priest casts holy water on the casket when it arrives at the church for the funeral. When I was growing up, all Catholic families had a little holy water font in the bedroom, and you blessed yourself before you went to sleep—or, if you were a kid, you warded off monsters under the bed with a well-aimed splash.

The holy water font is, of course, a miniature baptismal font designed to remind us that we are baptized. That, in turn, reminds us that we were initiated into discipleship with Jesus, we belong to Jesus. Baptism is our identification card, our mark, that tells the world whom we belong to, just as a brand on a cow does. We are sealed, signed, forever identified.

When we bless ourselves with water from the font, therefore, we are unconsciously reminding ourselves and the world that, as a matter of profound fact, we are baptized Christians. As I said, we do this so automatically that this thought is the farthest thing from our minds. But on this feast of the Baptism of Jesus, it might be well to remember that baptism, like membership in any organization or group, carries with it privileges, obligations, and expectations.

To share an example, I have chosen the true story of an exemplary priest—mostly, I guess, because the priesthood must now win back the love, respect, and, above all, the trust of the people. Well, this priest, Giuseppe Puglisi, never lost any of these. He gave himself so completely that before long he will be declared a martyr; in fact, his name was included in the centennial service held in the catacombs for martyrs of the twentieth century.

Giuseppe's father was a shoemaker, and his mother, a seamstress. He entered the seminary at the age of sixteen. One of his first assignments was to a rural parish torn apart by a bloody vendetta. He was then named pastor of the church of San Gaetano in a poor section of Palermo, in Sicily; at the same time he taught at a Catholic high school. His parish was no choice assignment: it was housed in an eighteenth-century church with the roof falling in. The parishioners numbered 115 in an area with a population of 8,000.

What distinguished Giuseppe as a priest was his heroic and fearless opposition to the Mafia. Films like *The Godfather* have given us a somewhat romantic view of the Mafia; but there is nothing romantic about a vicious criminal organization that, especially in Sicily, holds people in its power by threats and murder. The local politicians in Palermo were corrupted or in fear of them, but the priest was not. He refused to accept their donations for feast day celebrations. From the pulpit he denounced those who gave and accepted bribes, and he tried to move the municipality to decent levels of service.

But especially, Giuseppe worked with the youth. We are told that he organized camping trips for classes at the high school. At

San Gaetano's he hammered away at the same themes: take responsibility for your life and for society; resist the values of the Mafia: refuse to collaborate in their criminality; say no to contraband goods, to "discounted" (that is, stolen) motorbikes, and to drugs. His heroic stand had a price. On his fifty-sixth birthday, returning from a round of pastoral duties and a small birthday party, Fr. Giuseppe Puglisi stepped out of his car and was immediately shot in the head. The assailant, caught four years later, was a low-level Mafioso. He later reported that when Puglisi saw him approaching, he said quietly, "I was expecting you."

What a beautiful man! I was deeply struck by his last words on earth: "I was expecting you." I was struck because his words seemed to be the very essence of baptism, of what this sacrament is all about. It means that when you're initiated into the Christ-way of living and loving, and you take it seriously, there are certain expectations.

Archbishop Oscar Romero, who was assassinated while celebrating Mass, knew that his strong words on behalf of the poor and persecuted would bring reprisals. He actually forgave his assassins before the event because he was fully expecting that his baptismal commitment would bring them.

Martin Luther King, Jr., the Baptist minister, knew the same. He, too, expected to pay the price for his baptismal commitment. Today, this expectation translates in various ways:

"You blew the whistle on the company." "I know, but it was doing things to hurt people." "Nevertheless, you can't do such things and stay employed. You're fired." A pause and a sigh: "I was expecting you."

"Sorry, Jerry. There will be drinking and drugs and lots of sex at the party. You know that. Sorry to be the one to tell you that, with your scruples, you're not invited." "I was expecting you."

"Hey, Jane, so, we cut a few corners here and there. What's the big deal? You in or you out?" "I was expecting you."

That's the way it works—or is supposed to work. Sign yourself with the baptismal cross, and you'll automatically get the sacrificial cross. Of course, you can lay it down and erase the sign so that nobody even knows you're a Christian. You can be exactly like everybody else: formed by the media, with media values and lifestyles. For these people there are scriptural words from Jesus: "Not everyone who cries out 'Lord! Lord!' will enter the kingdom of heaven but only those who do the will of my Heavenly Father."

But those baptized Christians who sign themselves and mean it, who suffer because of their commitment, will hear these words from Jesus, words now full of new and glorious meaning: "I was expecting you."

Lent & Easter

The Desert Experience

Genesis 2:7–9; 3:1–7

At that time Jesus was led by the Spirit into the desert to be tempted by the devil…. The word of God came to John the Baptist in the desert…. In the desert Moses was confronted by God.

The desert has always been a symbol for the encounter between the naked self and God. That's because the desert is so bald, so barren, so vast, so primeval, so unforgiving, so basic, so hand-to-mouth that because one must concentrate on simply surviving, all distractions are filtered out, and one is left alone with oneself. Going into the desert, the desert journey, has become a metaphor for leaving all behind and, in our utter exposure and honesty, confronting who and what we are and what really matters. Often, going on a retreat or being laid low by illness is referred to as a desert experience.

The Church has its own version of a collective desert experience. It is called Lent. The season of Lent urges us to take some time apart from our day-to-day lives to reflect on three basics. But before I mention what these three basics are, we must first pay tribute to just how hard it is to stand apart and observe our everyday lives. As we well know, our society is not conducive to developing the interior life, to solitude, or to inner examination—in short, to the desert experience.

We know the problem all too well. The nearly 5,000 commercials we subliminally absorb every day; the constant noise that has become so commonplace and pervasive we don't even attend to it anymore; the persistent metronome that beats out the same message day after day, that always being busy and constantly on the go is the socially acceptable sign of being "with it," of being vigorous and successful. Then there is a capitalist system that considers rest unproductive; a relentless commercial media that hectors us to consume twenty-four hours a day—these are all powerful barriers to going into the desert. We are conditioned to abhor silence, solitude, and inactivity.

Yet, if the unexamined life is not worth living, as Socrates said, so the Church says neither is the un*reflective* life. So the Church urges us to come away awhile during Lent, to find some time for prayer, reflection, Scripture reading, perhaps a day of recollection or a mini-retreat—to encounter our three basics.

The first basic is our brokenness. None of us is whole. We are not wholly what we should be and what we were called by God to be. We know that, even though we seldom take time to reflect on this sorry state of ours. We know we have strayed from the moral life, the generosity, kindness, consideration, and decency that should be ours. Instead, we have been self-serving, mean, exploitative, and hurtful in thought, word, and deed, in what we have done and in what we have failed to do. Simply put, we are broken at moral places.

Unflinchingly, then, during Lent, we must take a look at that brokenness, however hard or unpleasant. We must encounter our moral emptiness. When rock singer Andy Gibb died at thirty years of age after years of substance abuse, his friends said that he had a great emptiness within. Too bad he never filled that emptiness with Jesus instead of drugs.

But others who are famous have chosen Jesus. Broadcaster Ted Turner has said that Christianity is for losers, for people who are weak and who cannot make it on their own. He has called the people he saw wearing ashes on Ash Wednesday "Jesus freaks." I am wondering if he's whistling a different tune now that he is divorced from Jane Fonda. Reportedly the divorce occurred because Ms. Fonda, one of the world's most independent women, has become a Christian and gladly dependent on

Christ. Presumably, she is now too weak to be his wife. Somewhere along the way her brokenness caught up with her, and as she went through the desert of another divorce and emptiness, she found Jesus.

The second basic we must encounter in our desert experience is our value system. We all have values that we live by even though we may never consciously spell them out or articulate them. But we surely live by them just as Hugh Hefner lives by his "values" and the people on *Sex in the City* and *The Sopranos* do. We all live by unspoken values; it's time to ask where we get them from. One clue comes from Jim Wallis, a very famous minister, who points out that a night in front of the television set can be an indoctrination into the seven deadly sins. We've got to do better than that.

Some here might remember the name Eldredge Cleaver. He was one of the best-known militants of the sixties, one of the most notorious members of the group known as the Black Panthers. But today, Eldredge Cleaver is a follower of Jesus. In his book *Soul on Fire*, Cleaver tells of his conversion and of a vision he had in one of his quiet, desert times. He writes:

I saw all my former heroes paraded before my eyes—Fidel Castro, Mao Tse Tung, Karl Marx, Frederick Engels—passing in review, each one appearing for a moment of time and then dropping out of sight, like fallen heroes. Finally, at the end of the procession, in dazzling, shimmering light, the image of Jesus Christ appeared.

Jesus challenged the destructive values Cleaver was living by and offered him another set of values. Lent is the time to check what values *we're* living by.

Finally, in our desert experience we must search for meaning and purpose. We can't just go along mindlessly dancing to the tune TV sets for us. We have a deeper reason for living than consuming things and people. The fundamental lenten questions concern meaning and purpose. What does God want of me? What is my mission? What is my calling? I instinctively know I have a deeper meaning and purpose, and I must seek it out. This means I need some quiet desert time to make that discovery. If I have found my meaning and purpose in counterfeit negative identities and have lived by them, I must repent and find the positive purpose given to me by God.

Baby Boomers will probably remember the name of the rock star Alice Cooper. (If you think Alice Cooper is a "she," you give your real age away!) Alice Cooper was one of the first "shock rock" acts. He used to parade on stage with gross makeup and live snakes and simulate his own decapitation—a pretty raunchy act, like KISS and other rock stars today who parade raunchiness and infantile sex as part of their acts.

Alice Cooper's long and successful career is the epitome of everything that critics hate about rock and roll. He has glorified rebellion, immorality, idolatry, and excess like practically no other rock artist. Considering all this, many people were surprised, even shocked, when Alice Cooper converted to Christianity. He discovered in his desert experience that all that excess and rebellion were masking his need to have a better, more noble purpose in life. So he gave his life over to Christ in 1995, and he is now involved in a church in Phoenix, Arizona. He even sings in the choir and volunteers at church dinners. Cooper is keeping a low profile and concentrating on growing in Christ and finding out what his next step should be as a disciple of Jesus.

Jane Fonda, Eldredge Cleaver, and Alice Cooper—an actress, a militant, and a rock star—are highly unlikely models, as I said before. But I suggest they are apt models for the lenten journey as we confront brokenness, false values, and the true purpose of life. Maybe it might be a good idea to spend one week of Lent on each topic, then the rest of the time before Easter earnestly praying for conversion. And, yes, I admit that it might be a stretch to add to our litany Saint Jane, Saint Eldredge, or Saint Alice. But since they're people who have met and accepted the lenten challenge, they might at least give us the encouragement to enter into the desert experience.

Choose

Mark 1:12–15

Last Sunday's newspaper will form the basis of our reflection for this first Sunday of Lent. It carried the stories of four people who, it turns out, represent the two paths in life.

The first is a man named Khalid Shaikh Mohammed. He is a leader of Al Qaeda and a close lieutenant of Osama Bin Laden. One of the world's most wanted terrorists and a chief suspect in the suicide attacks on the World Trade Center and the Pentagon, he has at last been captured and is now in American custody. His history is one of violence and destruction, yet this killer, this hater, this destroyer rates front-page coverage.

Then there is another person who did not rate front-page coverage, a man who, unlike Mohammed, gave a lifetime of beautiful days. In his cardigan sweaters and with an unwaveringly sincere gaze, he shared words of wisdom, care, and affirmation with children who were trying hard to live in a world full of surprises, some bad and some good. He helped them with the hard stuff of life, like divorce, disability, and even death. He is, of course, Mr. Rogers.

Fred Rogers' death received a short write-up on an inside page, I guess because he didn't preach hate and revenge. Rather, he told children that whatever their bad feelings, whatever the trouble, it is important and something you can talk about. He told the children, "I like to be told when you're going away. I like to be told if it's going to hurt." He reminded them, "No person in this whole world is a mistake. You can never go down the drain." He would close each television show with these words: "There's never been anybody exactly like you before, and there will never be anybody exactly like you in the future. You're the only one." For all children, especially those who seldom heard such things in their tiny lives, his words were balm and comfort. He was a Presbyterian minister. I wonder if the Catholic Church canonizes non-Catholics? It should.

Now I ask you to consider one of the most dramatic of the episodes reported by the media in the last year: the rescue of nine miners trapped in the Quecreek coal mine in central Pennsylvania last July. The nine men were trapped 240 feet below the surface of the earth, in a narrow, meandering mine that was rapidly flooding with water.

Within minutes their path back to the entrance of the mine, a mile away from where they were, was completely blocked with water. They knew that they could survive only if rescue workers were able to drill through that 240 feet of earth to reach them. The odds were highly stacked against their rescue. Yet remarkably, the rescue workers reached the mine on their first try and eventually drilled a second larger hole through which the exhausted and dazed miners were brought to safety three days after the flooding. It was heroic and dramatic.

As journalist Peter Boyle writes, the minute the ordeal ended and the nine were back on firm ground, reporters, lawyers, agents, producers, book authors, and star television anchors all converged on the miners and urgently offered each of them compelling inducements of fame and money. They were now no longer people confronting death. They were instantly reduced to commodities ready to be marketed.

Disney quickly paid the miners $1.35 million in a group deal for the movie rights about their story, each man instantly receiving the equivalent of four years pay for labor in the mines. They were offered endorsement prospects, speaking engagements, and even the possibility of litigation for what they had endured. Having escaped the gruesome agony of being trapped below the earth, the miners now risked becoming entrapped by other people's need to make money off them. From Pennsylvania, let's move to New Jersey. There were police officers blocking intersections and television news vans outside of Sacred Heart Church in Camden, but no lawyers, agents, producers, book agents, or star television anchors. Certainly Disney was not there offering contracts for *this* story. But the church and the streets were crowded to overflowing for the funeral of a sixty-nine-year-old woman who ironically, having spent the past sixteen years fighting poverty and drug use on the mean streets of Camden, wound up getting killed as a passenger in a car that was hit by man who had been smoking crack cocaine.

The woman's name was Sister Peg Hynes. She was totally dedicated to improving the lives and living conditions of the people in a poor neighborhood. One freelance reporter at the funeral said it all, I think, when he wrote this account:

I squeezed into the standing-room-only crowd inside the lovingly restored church just in time to catch my second glimpse of Sister Peg as her coffin was closed. Mourners that night heard a reading from the Book of Revelation, hymns sung in Vietnamese, and a heart-rending performance of *Danny Boy* on a lone violin. The Rev. Michael Doyle, the pastor of Sacred Heart, described his friend as a hammock strung between generosity and need who died in a clash of good and evil.

As a group of parishioners carried baskets of food for the needy to the altar for blessing, my eye fixed on an item in one of the baskets—a box of instant mashed potatoes. I found my self awed by the depth of the faith of Sister Peg and people like her, people who believe in God and a New Jerusalem in the hereafter but also believe that, with enough boxes of instant mashed potatoes for the needy and enough buckets of fresh paint on old houses, there can be a New Camden in the here and now.

The funeral Mass ended, and the congregation spilled out of the church into the night to walk in a procession through the neighborhood. Someone held up a single candle, which flickered above the mass of the crowd. At that moment, a dark and mean South Camden street became a scene of profound and subtle beauty.

Do I have to say anymore? I am going to go and sit down, as I usually do, to let you think about what I said—and to think about Lent, for Lent is written all over my words. I have presented both you and myself with two paths: the path of hate or the path of love; the path of selfishness or the path of service; the path of regression or the path of repentance; Mohammed or Mr. Rogers; Disney or Sister Peg.

Choose.

Lent Blesses

Genesis 12:1–4

"In you all the families of the earth shall be blessed."

The quotation above is from the book of Genesis. The full quotation, spoken to Abraham, is this:

> I will make of you a great nation, and I will bless you, and make your name great, so that you will be a blessing. I will bless those who bless you…and in you all the families of the earth shall be blessed.

Even though others might never have heard of him, Abraham was to be a blessing to others. In him, others would find their lives blessed, whether they realized it or not.

What a nice program for the followers of Jesus. What a good motto or life-theme. What a fine resolution for Lent. What a good core conviction to carry with us and to try to live by; that is, to be a blessing to others. This is our calling, our destiny. You and me, little, insignificant you and me—our vocation through baptism is to be a blessing to others, to bless others. And we, in turn, are to be gratefully conscious that others have blessed us, are blessing us every day of our lives even though we are not aware of it. And we must remember to show gratitude.

Let me give you a concrete example of a hidden blessing. I don't know if you know the story of Charles Plumb, who was a U.S. Navy jet pilot in Vietnam. After seventy-five combat missions, his plane was destroyed by a surface-to-air missile. Plumb ejected and parachuted into enemy hands. He was captured and spent six years in a Communist Vietnamese prison. Plumb survived the ordeal, and he now spends his time lecturing on the lessons he learned from that experience.

One day when Plumb and his wife were sitting in a restaurant, a man at another table came up and said excitedly, "You're Plumb! You flew jet fighters in Vietnam from the aircraft carrier Kitty Hawk! You were shot down!" "How in the world did you know that?" asked the amazed Plumb. The man replied, "I packed your parachute." Plumb gasped in surprise and gratitude. While he was recovering from his speechlessness, the man pumped his hand and said, "Well, guess it worked!" Plumb regained his composure and assured him, "It sure did. If your chute hadn't worked, I wouldn't be here today." And they parted.

End of coincidence, end of story? Not quite. You see, Plumb couldn't sleep that night. He kept thinking about that man. Plumb says:

> I kept wondering what he might have looked like back then in a Navy uniform: a white hat, a bib in the back, and bell-bottom trousers. I wonder how many times I might have seen him and not even said, "Good morning, how are you?" or anything because, you see, I was a fighter pilot, and he was just a sailor.

Plumb then began to think of the many hours that ordinary sailor had spent on a long wooden table in the bowels of the ship, carefully weaving the shrouds and folding the silks of each chute, holding in his hands each time the fate of someone he didn't know.

Having thought long and hard about this meeting, Plumb now asks his audience when he lectures, "Who's packing your parachute?" His point is that everyone has someone who has packed their parachutes, who has blessed them, who has provided what they need to make it through the day.

Plumb points out that in fact he needed many kinds of parachutes when his plane was shot down over enemy territory. He needed his physical parachute, his mental parachute, his emotional parachute, and his spiritual parachute. He called on all these supports before reaching safety. Somebody had put them there, had richly blessed him, and he was grateful and determined to pass on that blessing.

Tell me: who blessed you this week? Think about it. Who made your lunch, did your laundry, fixed your car, cleaned your streets, picked up your garbage, took your pulse, opened your door, waited on your table, brought your mail? Who blessed you today, yesterday? Who packed your parachute?

Then, of course, there's the lenten question: whose parachute have *you* packed? Or should have packed? Whom did you bless this week—or fail to bless? Sometimes, in the daily challenges that life gives us, we miss what is really important. We may fail to say hello, please, or thank you, congratulate someone on something wonderful that has happened to them, give a compliment, or just do something nice for no reason.

Remember: like Abraham, we are called to bless. It was also predicted of us: "In you all the families of the earth shall be blessed." Lent is the time to recall both how we are blessed and how we bless others. If there is a failure to bless, Lent is the time to repent, to confess, to promise to do better. Most of all, Lent is simply a time to recall our awesome Abrahamic vocation. We are here on earth to be a blessing to others. It's a deep calling.

And at judgment time, when Jesus asks, "And whose parachute did you pack?" it will be wonderful to be able to list a whole bunch of folks. Jesus, of course, will use other words even though they mean the same thing. He will say, "When I was hungry, you gave me to eat; when I was thirsty, you gave me to drink, when I was sick, you visited me...." It's the same thing, the same thought.

So what is the moral for Lent? Start packing parachutes, and start blessing those who packed yours.

Are We There Yet?

Genesis 12:1–4

A little boy was riding with his father from New Mexico to Colorado on a fishing trip. The trip covered 250 miles, a good five hours of driving—not counting rest and restaurant stops. After about thirty miles the excited son asked his father if they were almost there. The father answered that they had quite a ways to go.

Fifty miles later: "Now are we almost there?" asked the boy.

"No," said his father, "not yet."

Another fifty miles later: "We must be just about there, right, Daddy?"

"No," said his father, "not yet. We have about another hundred miles to go."

Fifty miles later, the lad inquired: "Daddy, am I still going to be four years old when we get there?"

That is my introduction to the Abraham story found in today's first reading. This old man, from whom three faiths derive—Judaism, Islam, and Christianity—was a nomad, a wanderer. Not, as you know, by choice; he was summoned suddenly from his comfortable life and old, familiar neighborhood. He was asked to leave his friends, along with everything he knew and cherished, and told to set out for the unknown, for a land he knew nothing about or how to get there or what dangers might await him on the way—and there were many. He had no Mapquest or OnStar, only God's word and God's promise. He must have asked many times, "Are we there yet?"

But Abraham is not the only one who is on a journey not of his own choosing. Like Abraham, all of us are called again and again to leave the safe and familiar, the sound and the sane, to venture into territories unknown, uncharted, and unsure. It starts early. As infants, we are called to leave the safety of the womb to be born into an often unfriendly world. Sooner or later we leave the cozy cocoon of home for the first day of school—remember that? Then we leave the comfortable routine of school for our first job; then we leave our mother and father, brothers and sisters, to cling to a spouse and begin a family of our own; then we leave our hometown to move to where the work is, perhaps many times. Then one day—it comes so soon!—we leave work for retirement. And then, somewhere along the line, we leave our own home for a senior citizen village or a convalescent home or hospice care; finally, we leave the relative security of this world for one we do not know.

It seems that's what life is about: we're always on an adventure, on a journey, whether we want to be or not. We are forever leaving and arriving, arriving and leaving. Life doesn't stand still. In the depths of our being, we are all nomads, all Abrahams and Sarahs, all wanderers for a time on the journey of life. With all these arrivals and departures in life, the nomadic Abraham and Sarah are offered as our models for Lent, and for two reasons. First, they travelled trusting that God would sustain them. Second, they took time out along the way to entertain angels—that is, to do good deeds—and as a result, they grew in faith along the way.

Let me remind you that Lent is precisely the time to look into our spiritual lives and see if we have grown in faith along the way. It's a time to pause and ask life's profound questions: what does my life journey look like so far? Am I where I should be at this stage of my life? Am I making progress as a human being, as a saint? Have I entertained angels? And, dare we ask it: am I holier now than I was at this time last year? Have I grown spiritually, or have I simply grown physically older but not better, or more gentle, or more forgiving, or more compassionate?

Let me tell you about a woman named Rose who captivated her fellow students from the very first day of college. Why? Because Rose, like Abraham and Sarah, was old, eighty-seven years old to be precise! When asked, "Why are you in college at such an age?" she would jokingly reply, "I'm here to meet a rich husband, get married, have a couple of children, and then retire and travel." But when serious, she said, "I always dreamed of having a college education, and now I'm getting one!" Well, the students were mesmerized listening to this "time machine" as she shared her wisdom and experience over the course of the school year. Eventually Rose became a campus icon who easily made friends wherever she went.

At the end of the semester, Rose was so popular that she was invited to speak at the football banquet. She was introduced and stepped up to the podium. As she began to deliver her pre-pared speech, she dropped her three-by-five notecards on the floor. Frustrated and a little embarrassed, she leaned into the microphone and said, "I'm sorry I'm so jittery. I gave up beer for Lent, and this whiskey is killing me!"

After the laugher died down, she said, "Look, I'll never get my speech back in order so let me just tell you what I know." She then got serious and proceeded to say things like: "We do not stop playing because we are old; we grow old because we stop playing," and, "You've got to have a dream. When you lose your dreams, you die." Then, most impressively, she said, "There is a huge difference between growing older and growing up. Anybody can grow older. That doesn't take any talent or ability. The idea is to grow up by always finding the opportunity in change. Growing older is mandatory; growing up is optional."

Good wisdom. And it sounds like a fine lenten theme, does-n't it? Like Abraham and Sarah, Rose has reminded us that we are all growing older with each tick of the clock. That, alas, is mandatory. The real challenge is whether we are growing up spiritually; *that* is optional.

Or, if you want to put in terms of our story at the beginning, like the little boy, we ask, "Earthly daddy, will we still be four years old—or forty years old—when we get there?" The answer, in terms of years, is "yes, of course." Age is mandatory. "Heavenly Daddy—Abba, Father—will we be spiritually grown up when we get there?" The answer, in terms of the Spirit, is "it all depends." Growth is optional.

Lent is a time to exercise our options.

The Honeymoon

Mark 9:2–10

"Honeymoon": the two words that compose it tell its story. The first month of marriage is the sweetest—the "honey" part. But then comes the "moon," at first full and bright, and eventually, it wanes. So does the initial affection of a married couple. And we all comment, "The honeymoon is over." What was Roger Dangerfield's one-liner? "There she was when I first saw her, the loveliest girl on the dance floor. Then she got up." It's just like the first months a newly elected president is in office, when he and Congress are cordial to each other; or a new manager who is all smiles at first and then one day the honeymoon is over as differences and adjustments arise.

Only the immature, the really spiritually immature—like some child stars or celebrities or those who watch too much television—think that the honeymoon can and should last forever. So in vain they work hard to preserve it. Constantly reshaping themselves with cosmetic surgery to look like the current idol, popping Viagra and diet pills, totally devoted to makeovers, wearing the right clothes, being seen with the right people, projecting a cool image, they strive to do the impossible: to hold on to the honeymoon, the moment, the youth, the frozen image of perfection, bliss, and desirability, to always stay on top; to be Joe Millionaire forever.

But, as most common-sense folk know, life isn't lived only on top. It's lived in the hills of monotony, in the fields of work, in the valleys of disappointments, and, mostly, on the plains of quiet devotion, love, and sacrifice, which in the end bring one full circle to a depth of love never envisaged nor even possible on the honeymoon. If you've ever met devoted golden jubilarians, you know what real love is like.

But the temptation to settle into fantasy land, to dream of remaining forever young and desirable, to idolize and freeze the fifteen minutes of fame, is great; and it is highly promoted by an advertising industry that endlessly promises to eliminate all odors, pains, wrinkles, sadness, aging, death, and difficult decisions—for a price, of course.

As you just heard in the gospel, Peter succumbed to this temptation. Dazzled by the mountaintop transfiguration, he exclaimed, "Let's settle in here and build a couple of cottages and live happily ever after." But it was not to be, could not be, and he was hit with that most realistic of sentences found in today's gospel: "Suddenly when they looked around, they saw no one with them any more, but only Jesus." That was it. Just like that, it was all gone: the celebrities, Moses and Elijah; the voice from the cloud, the dazzle, the strobe lights. Only Jesus was left, and he matter-of-factly spoke of death as they came down the mountain, off the honeymoon.

Jesus was speaking about taking up your cross daily to follow him, which is to say, make your crucial decisions to be faithful and chaste, honest and trustworthy, just, merciful, and forgiving in the everyday-ness of life. The celebrity moments are nice; enjoy them, but don't get stuck there for they do not last, nor are they meant to last. Rather, get busy with the unglamorous, mundane graces: feed the hungry, give drink to the thirsty, clothe the naked, counsel the doubtful, instruct the ignorant, give alms, visit the sick, tell the truth, and keep your vows. And beware of the false prophets who promise you endless honeymoons and mountaintops. Life, grace, and redemption are lived and gained in the plains.

Let me share an example of this. One of the greatest mountaintop experiences ever recorded happened on May 19, 1953. That was the day when Edmund Hillary and his native Sherpa guide, Tenzing Norgay, reached the top of Mount Everest. They were the first two people ever to be literally on top of the world, somewhat like Peter, James, and John. After Hillary had climbed Mount Everest, he became what most people think they desire most of all in life: he became an overnight celebrity. He was knighted by Queen Elizabeth. His name became a household word, which to most Scandinavians is even better than being knighted. He achieved celebrity status as his name appeared as a logo on sleeping bags, tents, and boot laces. You can't do better than that.

Edmund Hillary could have tried to live in his little dwelling of success for the rest of his life. But he knew better. He knew that life is not really lived on top. So what did he do? He went back to little, out-of-the-way Nepal. Back to the Sherpas, whom he had grown to know and appreciate and respect and love. And he used his fame to bring them help.

In a speech given some years ago, Hillary recounted how an elderly Sherpa from Khumjung village, the hometown of most of the Sherpas on his Everest ascent, had come to him a few years after that expedition and said, "Our children lack education. They are not prepared for the future. What we need more than anything is a school in Khumjung." So Hillary established the Himalayan Trust, and in 1961 a three-room schoolhouse was built in Khumjung with funds raised by Hillary. In its first decade the fund focused on education and health. Since then, the trust has built twenty-seven schools, two hospitals, and twelve medical clinics, plus numerous bridges and airfields. They are also involved in the reforestation of valleys and slopes in many areas of Nepal.

Hillary spent more than half the year traveling the world, raising money for the trust and supervising its various projects. And he has continued to do this for more than thirty years. Many people today don't know Edmund Hillary. He's no longer a household word—he's certainly no match for Jennifer Lopez or Eminem—and you won't find him endorsing products. His monument is not written on plaques or sewn on clothing labels, but in the countless hearts of happy children. After his fifteen minutes of fame with the world, he has eternal fame with a grateful people and a loving God.

This second Sunday of Lent says, enjoy the transfiguring times of your life, but don't spend all your time trying to cultivate your image on the outside. In spite of the terrible tyranny of advertising that dictates that you simply must have the latest "in" thing to be a worthwhile and acceptable person, spend your time this Lent on making the inside better.

Be a better, more noble person. Take some of the energy that goes into burnishing your exterior image and build the interior life. Dedicate yourself to prayer and the everyday-ness of the corporal and spiritual works of mercy. Give alms. Visit the sick. Forgive enemies. You really don't need another sweater or the latest CD. Give that money to the poor. This is a surer and better way to maturity, wholeness, and holiness.

What's the bottom line? The honeymoon is wonderful, but the moon must wane. The mountaintop is exhilarating, but the plain is where it's at. Hobnobbing with celebrities like Moses and Elijah is nifty, but serving your neighbor gets you to heaven. The transfiguration is a lift, but being alone with Jesus is what counts.

Zeal for Your House

John 2:13–15

Jesus came, saw, and acted exclaiming, "Zeal for your house has consumed me," as he spun his homemade whip. He found some things intolerable, like desecrating a sacred temple with cheap commercialism. The best modern version of his attitude occurs in that very sharp movie *Network*, where, you recall, actor Peter Finch shouts, "I'm mad as hell, and I'm not going to take it anymore!"

And here is a lenten question for us that we don't often think about: what gets our moral dander up, or, more ominously, what doesn't and should? After all, we will be judged on our moral crusades. Lent is a time to take a look at what makes us morally mad to the point of doing something about it—or to look at our failure to get mad and do something about it. Offhand, I can think of two seldom mentioned issues that should attract our zeal and anger.

Issue one, sadly, comes from our local paper. The other day a large headline read, "Point Boro soccer star found dead." It told the story of a twenty-three-year-old college student who was found dead by his roommates, and a preliminary investigation points to an alcohol and/or drug overdose.

I don't know how it began for this young man, God rest him and comfort his family. But I wonder if he was among the thirty percent of high school students whom the Center for Disease Control say have engaged in "episodic heavy drinking" within the last thirty days. That means they each had five or or more drinks in a row on one or more occasions during the month.

In a University of Michigan survey conducted last year, thirty percent of high school seniors reported being drunk a least once in the past thirty days. Nationally, the average age at which young people now start drinking has dropped to fourteen. I don't know if this twenty-three-year-old started out that way, but I do know that Joseph Califano, Jr., president of the National Center for Addiction and Substance Abuse (CASA), has shown that there is a link between the use of alcohol, nicotine, marijuana, and the move to harder drugs especially among teens. He reports that "Teens who have used cigarettes or alcohol within the last month are thirty times likelier to smoke pot. Those who have used all three of those are sixteen times likelier to move to hard drugs like cocaine."

But listen to this part of his report:

CASA's nine years of research have resulted in three conclusions. One, an individual who gets through the age of twenty-one without smoking, using illegal drugs, or abusing alcohol is virtually certain never to do so. Two, parent power is the most underused tool in the battle against substance abuse. And three, spirituality and religion are key factors in prevention and treatment. CASA has found that the more engaged parents are in their lives, the less likely children are to smoke, drink, or use illegal drugs. Involvement as basic as eating dinner with the children has an enormous impact on reducing drug use.

Now you might think that I am suggesting that you get morally mad at so much alcohol and drug abuse, along with its attendant crimes and personal devastations. Yes, of course I suggest that; but I really have something deeper in mind, something closer to home. I suggest that you get angry if you are not eating dinner as a family. By all accounts, parental presence is truly powerful beyond measure in deterring drug abuse. You should get mad if you haven't exercise that power. You should get angry enough to do something about it for Lent and thereafter.

Issue two: these are statistics from the U.S. Department of Health and Human Services, and they tell us about our own backyard:

- Nearly 104,000 people in Monmouth and Ocean counties live on incomes too low to provide their families with the basic necessities and face the "heat or eat" dilemma; that is, whether to pay the rent, pay the utilities, or buy food.

- A minimum-wage worker ($5.15 per hour) in Monmouth or Ocean county would have to work eighteen hours a day, seven days a week, to be able to afford the rent on an average two-bedroom apartment.

To move beyond where we live, attend carefully to this unnerving comparison. If the earth's entire population shrank to a village of one hundred people, with all of the human ratios remaining the same, what would that little village look like? Answer: in that little village, six of the one hundred inhabitants would be from the United States, and they would possess fifty-nine percent of the total wealth. Eighty would live in substandard housing, seventy would be unable to read, and fifty would be suffering from malnutrition.

To put it another way, if you have food in your fridge, clothes on your back, a roof over head, and a place to sleep, you are richer than seventy-five percent of the world's population. This means, let's say, that the first eight pews on one side of the middle aisle possess almost sixty percent of the wealth of this entire congregation. Half of us here would be suffering from malnutrition; almost three-quarters of the people in this church would be unable to read and after Mass would go home to substandard housing.

We know this sort of thing in our heads but not in our hearts, and that's understandable. You and I don't know many—if any—poor people, and we have probably never met one face to face. We're not heartless or uncaring; quite the contrary. It's just that the poor are invisible and are kept that way by a massive advertising industry that keeps us focused on glamorous images, designer labels, and endless consumption. You and I are blindsided by the 5,000 needs-creating commercials we see everyday that simply leave us no time to see the poor. Certainly we have no mental room left for imagining ourselves as one of those six out of one hundred people who have sixty percent of the entire wealth of the world; or that, moderate folk as we are, we are nevertheless richer that seventy-five percent of the world's population.

The poor were clearly the center of the Christian experience in the early centuries of the Church. In the fourth century, St. Gregory of Nyssa taught that in feeding and caring for the poor, we care for Christ. Christians are not owners of their goods, said his contemporary, St. Basil, but only administrators for the needs of others. The great model, the celebrity of the time, was St. Martin of Tours, who cut his cloak in half to give to a poor beggar. We've come a long way from that standard in our consumer society today. Not, I repeat, that we are any less generous or compassionate: we are abundantly both. It's just that alcohol abuse, drugs, and poverty are off our moral radar screen. Today's gospel says we should put them back and get angry enough to do something.

A few years ago, an eleven-year-old boy named Trevor Ferrell was shocked by the plight of the homeless on the streets of Philadelphia. He took a blanket and pillow from his own bed and asked his parents to drive him into the city, where he gave the bedding to the first homeless person he saw. Over time, his generosity became known, and contributions from corporations and churches began to augment his simple act of kindness. Social services, medical assistance, and legal aid were volunteered, and within a year, "Trevor's Place" was opened as a home for the homeless.

As today's gospel suggests, Lent is about seeing and examining what we get morally angry about—or fail to. There's an alcohol and drug problem out there, a big one. So let's get mad enough about it to eat dinner together for Lent. There is poverty right at our back door, closer than we think. Even here in New Jersey, some kids don't have enough to eat. Asbury Park and Camden and other places like that really exist. Let's all get mad enough—adults, teens, and kids—to give ten percent of our income, our allowance, to charity for Lent and then thereafter.

When Lent is over and resurrection time is at hand, we want to be able to stand happily before the Lord with a banner that proudly proclaims, "Zeal for your house has consumed me!"

Blindness and Sight

John 9:1–41

There are two kinds of blindness in Scripture: physical blindness and spiritual blindness. Let me give you an example of each.

In the year 1818, Louis was a nine-year-old boy whose father was a harness maker in France. The boy loved to watch his father work with leather. "Some day, Father," said Louis, "I want to be a harness maker, just like you." "Why not start now?" said his father, who took a piece of leather and drew a design on it. "Now, my son," he said, "take the hole-puncher and hammer and follow this design. Be careful that you don't hit your hand." The excited young boy began to work but, when he hit the hole-puncher, it flew out of his hand and pierced his eye! He immediately lost the sight of that eye. A few years later, his other eye failed. Louis was now totally blind.

One day, Louis was sitting in the family garden, and a friend handed him a pine cone. As Louis ran his fingers over the pine cone, an idea came to him. He began to create an alphabet of raised dots on paper so that blind people could feel the letters and read. In this way Louis Braille opened up a whole new world for the blind, and it came out of a tragic accident. It's not good to be blind or to suffer from any affliction. But we know that God can use people like Louis Braille or the blind man in today's gospel to bring enormous good to others. God can be glorified, and we can be richly blessed through suffering and pain.

Then there is spiritual blindness. Several years ago, the New York *Times* magazine published an article about a group of more than one hundred women, all Cambodian refugees who fled their country during the regime of Pol Pot, to escape the atrocities of the killing fields. Now living in Long Beach, California, every one of these women is certifiably blind—even though leading opthamologists insist that their eyes are not injured and are capable of functioning normally. Suffering from what has been determined to be hysterical blindness, these sightless women were so traumatized by the horrors of what they had witnessed that their bodies set up a protective barrier as it were, which also prevents them from seeing anything at all.

We all know people like that. Maybe they are not physically blind, but they are spiritually blind. We say that they just won't see or that they have tunnel vision. Their minds are set and made up, and they shut their minds and hearts to anything else. Sometimes they shut out God because they've suffered a traumatic loss, like the loss of a child, and they can't reconcile that event with a good God. Or, with shock, sadness, and disgust, they read about the pedophile scandals and, rightfully so, lose trust in God's church. Some people, because of their mindset, see only the bad, not the good; only the corruption, not the promise; only darkness, not light.

How will they see again? The answer is that only the faith witness of compassion and love will give them sight again. Let me tell you about Dr. Diane Komp. She is a pediatric oncologist who describes herself as an agnostic or even an atheist when she first entered the medical field. But working with dying children gave Dr. Komp an unshakable faith in God. She tells of a typical case from her early years: seven-year-old Anna had fought leukemia for five years, and she had no more strength left. But moments before she died, the little girl suddenly sat up in bed and announced that she saw angels. A smile lit up her face as she described their beautiful singing. And then this little child, radiant with joy, laid down and died. The doctor became alive in faith because of the witness of a child.

The truth is that we all are blind to some degree; all of us. We all have honest questions and lingering doubts. We wonder, for example, where is God in our lives? Or is he there at all? We wrestle with the problem of evil: how God could permit September 11th? Why do evil people prosper? Why do bad things happen to good people? Why do we have to die? The only thing we have to cling to is God's word that, as St. Paul has written, "No eye has seen, nor ear heard, nor the human heart conceived, what God has prepared for those who love him."

This story I am about to tell you has the same message. When William Montague Dyke was ten years old, he was blinded in an accident. Despite his disability, William graduated from a university in England with high honors. While he was in school, he fell in love with the daughter of a high-ranking British naval officer, and they became engaged.

Shortly before the wedding, William had eye surgery in the hope that the operation would restore his sight. If it failed, he would remain blind for the rest of his life. William insisted on keeping the bandages on his face until his wedding day. If the surgery was successful, he wanted the first person he saw to be his new bride.

The wedding day arrived. The many guests—including royalty, cabinet members, and distinguished men and women of society—assembled together to witness the exchange of vows. William's father, Sir William Hart Dyke, and the doctor who performed the surgery stood next to the groom, whose eyes were still covered with bandages.

The organ trumpeted the wedding march, and the bride slowly walked down the aisle to the front of the church. As soon as she arrived at the altar, the surgeon took a pair of scissors out of his pocket and cut the bandages from William's eyes. Tension filled the room. The congregation of witnesses held their breath as they waited to find out if William could see the woman standing before him. As he stood face-to-face with his bride-to-be, William's words echoed throughout the cathedral, "You are more beautiful than I ever imagined!"

I think that story is our heart's desire and faith's promise: that one day, when the bandages that cover the eyes of our mortal minds and hearts are removed, and we stand face-to-face with Jesus Christ and see him for the very first time, we will affirm what faith has promised: "You are more beautiful than I ever imagined."

The Clubhouse

Ephesians 2:4–10

As Lent winds down, and we face another Palm Sunday and Holy Week, it is appropriate to ask, why do we need Lent? A little parable gives the answer. Listen.

Once upon a time, a group of caring people from a seaside town decided to build a lighthouse to bring guidance and safety to their stormy coast. They built it high, and they built it strong to withstand the weather, and its bright beacon burned proudly through the darkness of the night. The town folks who maintained the station gathered each evening to tend the light. As they worked, they shared stories of the ships and people they had saved and of the service they had done.

At one point, they decided that the inside of their lighthouse could use some improvement. So they added a new rug, comfortable furniture, and a roaring fire. It made the lighthouse a cozy place for them to meet and to share each other's company.

One night, as the lighthouse tenders were gathered inside, the beacon light began to dim. But safe and warm from the darkness and storm, they didn't bother to tend it. After all, refugees from the wind and weather only tracked mud and water all over their new carpet. Finally, one night as the caring people shared the warmth and friendship that flourished inside the lighthouse, the great beacon light went out. But by then no one noticed, and no one much cared. It remained only to label what had happened.

Eventually, the lighthouse keepers took down the sign that

read "Lighthouse" and replaced it with a shiny new one that read, more truthfully, "Clubhouse."

The scriptural equivalent of this story is to be found in the book of Revelation where the angel confronts the people of various cities and, after enumerating their virtues, drops an indictment of their vices. In one such city the angel list its virtues but then adds, "But I have this against you: you have left your first love."

Indeed we have: the little compromises, the home turned into a building the size of a hotel, the car into a statement of power, the things that slowly have displaced people, the love of God grown cold, minor heroisms passed up, original ideals rerouted and forgotten. In short, the barnacles of life have accumulated, and suddenly we find that, you know, we do have a magnificent clubhouse, but somehow it's hard to find the lighthouse anymore. Somehow our moral light has dimmed, and we no longer serve others.

Our light is no longer a beacon for others who are looking for guidance on how to live in such an uncertain, fragile, and dangerous world as our own, where families disintegrate, corporate crime abounds, terrorism stalks, and our young are waging war in a foreign land. People know instinctively that clubhouses will not save them. In these uncertain times, they are looking for lighthouses to help them see the way. Once in while, in fact, people's hard sought-after clubhouses do come tumbling down, and a lighthouse is reclaimed. That happened literally when the World Trade Center collapsed.

It happened morally, too. On September 12, 2001, Genelle Guzman-McMillan became the last person to be rescued alive from the wreckage of the Trade Center's twin towers. No one yet understands how she was lucky enough to survive when more than 2,800 people who were in the same building at the same time died. Before the attacks on the World Trade Center, Genelle was a modern young woman living with her boyfriend, Roger. Genelle cared a lot about her appearance—the clubhouse on the outside, not the lighthouse on the inside—and about going out dancing with her friends. Occasionally, she and Roger attended church; once in a while they questioned whether there was more to life than work and club-hopping. But while she was trapped for twenty-six hours in the rubble of the World Trade Center, Genelle prayed fervently to God. She knows that God saved her.

After her release from the hospital, she and Roger married. They regularly attend church now. Genelle has not returned to work, but she has gained newfound faith in Jesus. Her priorities have changed. She believes that God saved her for a reason, and she wants urgently to understand what that reason is. She's rebuilding her life and is determined to make it a lighthouse.

Turning to someone who is more well-known, in 1999, best-selling author Stephen King was hit by a car while out walking near his home. The accident left him with severe injuries. In an article in *Family Circle* magazine, King writes that having a close brush with death taught him to contemplate the real meaning of life:

> I want you to consider making your life one long gift to others. And why not? All you have is on loan, anyway. All that lasts is what you pass on….Giving isn't about the receiver or the gift but the giver. It's *for* the giver. One doesn't open one's wallet to improve the world, although it's nice when that happens; one does it to improve one's self. I give because it's the only concrete way I have of saying that I'm glad to be alive.

Stephen King is determined to be a lighthouse.

Well, you get the drift. We have all left our first love. We have been busy, and our clubhouses are a testimony to our success. But Lent comes along and offers the challenge: we intended to make our business, our marriage, our family, our lives a lighthouse for others. When did we turn these things into a clubhouse for ourselves? The need to ask this question is more urgent than ever. In these tense and uncertain times, people are seeking. You know that as well as I do. They're looking to you and me who go to church, who represent Church. They want to find some guidance, some reassurance. They want a sign that God is here. They are in darkness. You have to show them a light to see by. We need Lent to tear down and rebuild, to move our souls from being clubhouses to being lighthouses.

We have two more weeks to complete the job.

Keeping Faith

John 20:19–31

"These are written so that you may come to believe...."

Perhaps it's just as well that we have this familiar Thomas story about belief and faith while we, as a Church, are still struggling with the worst scandal we've had since the Church came to the New World. People are disheartened, angry, weary of the daily headlines and exposes, appalled at the revelations about the priests and bishops they once held high on a pedestal. All is in disarray.

There is the loss of trust in the Church and the loss of respect. The Church has lost its moral capital. How can people listen seriously to the Church's teaching on abortion and chastity when its priests are unchaste? How can people take the Church's admirable teachings on social justice to heart when it has been unjust to pedophile victims? How can the Church's stance as a moral leader endure in the face of the scandals? How can people give credence to the Church's teaching on family life, as well as the care and the education of children, when it let its own children be violated? As for respect, the press has relentlessly paraded the sins of the Church before the public. The mainstream magazines and newspapers have made the scandal daily front page fare, and even a year later, the tabloid magazines and newspapers delight in revealing first-person horror stories.

The political cartoonists have had a field day pillorying

priests and bishops with cartoons ranging from the vulgar to the salacious. The sins of the priests and the "corruption" of Catholic Church have become the *scandal de jour*. The once-vaunted respect for the Church has evaporated. Its priests, tainted by the sins of their brothers, feel the stares and suspicions of others.

It's enough to make the people lose faith, like Thomas.

But do you know what? The remarkable thing is that the people haven't lost faith. I knew it was so when I spotted this headline in the *New York Times* on Easter Sunday: "Parish Embraces a Time of Hope, Not Scandal." It went on to tell about the parishioners of a parish in Wisconsin who, aware of and fretting over the scandals of so many abusive priests, were in church to draw a renewed faith from the themes of Holy Week. The sense of deceit, abandonment, betrayal, and death were there, all too familiar. But there was also the resurrection; this was Easter, and, indeed, they were there to embrace hope.

In fact, all around the country, the churches this Easter were more full than ever. Remarkably, though they may be sad and angry, the people are still keeping faith. Many simply love the Church and would never dream of leaving it. A few have said their faith was shaken. Some remarked that a priest or a bishop or a cardinal is only human. Others were glad that many priests raised the subject at Holy Week and Easter Masses.

Most often, people talked about the Church in terms of family and said things like: it's a dysfunctional family, and we've got to fix it; or it's like arguments among troubled relatives, but no one's ready to disown the family; or after all, it's Holy Mother Church, and even when your mother errs or you get angry with her, she's still your mother, and you're bound to her with lasting ties. I wonder if the bishops are listening. Do they realize they have such stalwart, faithful people who make better distinctions than they realize? I am reminded here of a great man of decades ago, Frank Sheed, father, author, and theologian, who was privy to many secrets in the Church. With an eye to history, he wrote on behalf of us all. Listen:

We are not baptized into the hierarchy; do not receive the cardinals sacramentally; will not spend an eternity in the beatific vision of the pope. St. John Fisher could say in a public sermon, "If the pope will not reform the curia, God will." A couple of years later, he laid his head on Henry VIII's block for papal supremacy; followed to the same block by Thomas More, who had spent his youth under the Borgia pope, Alexander VI; lived his early manhood under the Medici pope, Leo X; and died for papal supremacy under Clement VIII, as time-serving a pope as Rome ever had.

Christ is the point. I myself admire the present pope, but even if I criticized him as harshly as some do, even if his successor proved to be as bad as some of those who have gone before, even if I sometimes find the Church as I have to live with it, a pain in the neck, I should still say that nothing a Pope [or a priest] could do or say would make me wish to leave the Church, although I might well wish that they would leave. Israel, through its best periods as through its worst, preserved the truth of God's oneness in a world swarming with gods and a sense of God's majesty in a world sick with its own pride. So with the Church. Under the worst administration we could still learn Christ's truth, receive his life in the sacraments, be in union with him to the limit of our willingness. In awareness of Christ I can know the Church as his mystical body, and we must not make our judgment by the neck's sensitivity to pain.

Frank Sheed has it right. That's why you're here this morning. I think people have an instinctive appreciation of this truth. No one—no pope, no bishop, no priest—can completely erase the face of Christ or undo his mission. Grace is still amazing even among the revelations of scandal. Renewal is larger than sin, faith is stronger than scandal, hope is deeper than despair. Jesus is simply too strong, too "risen" to be undone by a new set of Judases.

I think people like yourself have the same unspoken belief that, as Frank Sheed said, Christ is the point, not this or that priest. It is to your credit that, hurt by the publicity, wounded by a breach of trust, plagued by doubt, and scandalized by betrayal, you can still come here today and steadfastly say with Thomas, "My Lord and my God."

It is with such faith that reform and renewal will happen.

Thomas

John 20:19–31

The world was surprised when Mother Teresa's diary was made public, and people read about her painful doubts. Was her work right? Did God care? Was there a God after all? It turns out this holy woman, now on her way to official sainthood, was plagued with many religious doubts.

But this Sunday, when we read about Thomas, the quintessential gospel doubter, we should remember that everyone walks through life with doubt on one arm and faith on the other. Sometimes one pulls harder than the other. Most human beings follow the tug of faith. To illustrate, imagine that you're in a shopping mall, and a group of college students asks you to participate in an experiment for their psychology class. You agree and allow them to blindfold you and place a cardboard box at your feet pressing against your toes. They then ask you to ascertain, without removing the blindfold, if the box is empty or contains a live Easter rabbit. How might you go about it?

There are basically three ways to approach. You could bend down and stick your hand into the box and feel around to determine if there is a rabbit inside. This would be gaining knowledge by direct experience, through the use of your senses. Second, you could pick up the box and judge from its weight or shake it to detect motion. This would be gaining knowledge through reasoning or deduction. Third, you could simply call out to someone passing by and ask if there is a rabbit in the box. This would be learning by believing or placing faith in the testimony of someone else. Of the three ways of gaining knowledge, which one do you think is the most important and the one most often used? If you answered "faith," accepting the word of another, you would be correct. Scientists say we gain more than seventy-five percent of all our knowledge by accepting the word of others.

Think about it: I always look at the nutritional value on the food packages I buy, yet I have no way of checking if the fat content and cholesterol percentages listed are accurate. I just accept the testimony of the label. I take it on faith. I've never been to the North Pole or to Iraq, but I believe they exist on the word of the people who say they have been there. The last time you flew, did you check to see if the pilot had his license? You just took it on faith that he did. Am I a real priest or a clerical Professor Howard Hill? Not one of you has ever asked to see my credentials.

So it goes. The scientists are right. We *do* accept most of our knowledge on faith. But doubt always lurks, as it must, whenever we do not have direct knowledge ourselves. And doubts about religion, our faith, are commonplace, as they too must be. It's part of being human. We have questions about the credibility of our witnesses. Furthermore, cramped by a modern mindset, we have intellectual doubts as we wonder if miracles occur, the gospels are true, Jesus is divine, God exists, or if the Church, with its present scandals, can claim any right to be called the Church of Jesus Christ. Our emotional doubts increase in proportion when we are sorely afflicted: where was God when my daughter was killed or my husband died or my son was in an accident that left him paralyzed—especially when I have been so faithful? Couldn't God have treated his own better?

It's something, I guess, like Thomas. It was all right up to a point, but when his best friend and mentor, this innocent man who went around doing good, was cruelly arrested, beaten, disfigured, and horribly crucified, how could he believe in God anymore? When people have intellectual or emotional doubts about faith—and most do—there are few answers. But there *are* three practical approaches we can take. Let's examine them.

First, stay with community. You notice that when Thomas was off by himself, his doubts got the better of him. Only when he rejoined the community was he able to say, "My Lord and my God." The fact is no one believes all the time; no one can feel God's presence all the time. But the community does. The community believes when you and I are unwilling or unable to do so. Peter believed for Doubting Thomas until he could believe again. Thomas believed for Denying Peter until he could embrace again. Monica believed for her son Augustine when he was in his period of sinfulness and doubt until he could repent again. Clare believed for Francis when he was sad until he was glad again.

We are a gathering of Christians. We support each other, and as a faith community, we become more than the sum total of our individual selves. You exhibit the gifts I don't have, and I exhibit those you don't have. You cry the tears I cannot cry, and I laugh the laughter you cannot laugh. You believe when I struggle with doubts; I believe when you struggle with doubts. Our individual pieces are partial. Our faith, our hope, and our love are quite incomplete. But we belong to a vast community of time and space, and the mighty truth is this: together we believe more than we believe alone. That is why, even with our doubts, we should stick with community.

Second, when doubt becomes strong, and the temptation to drop out is severe, resist it. The path of the "painful pilgrim" is the way to go. Come to church. This stance is sometimes confused with hypocrisy, but it is different. The hypocrite is one who consciously is pretending to be better than he or she is, saying one thing and doing another. The painful pilgrim knows he or she is in a period of doubt and unbelief but sticks with going to church, not in order to deceive, but to continue the search in order to be there the next time Christ reappears in his or her life. The painful pilgrim, unlike the hypocrite but like Mother Teresa, is a noble person.

Third, experience faith people. If your diet is *People* magazine, MTV, and pop culture—in short, if your intellectual and emotional diet is a steady intake of secular sources that are fundamentally sneering, skeptical, and unbelieving—then sooner or later, the old adages come true: "Birds of a feather flock together," and "Tell me who your friends are, and I will tell you who you are." If your steady "friends" are freewheeling hedonists, scoffers, lovely and engaging agnostics, bright secularists, then your doubts will sink deeper and deeper without the counterbalance of faith-filled people. Belief does not survive well in faithless company anymore that resistance to drugs survives well among drug-taking friends. It's as commonsensibly simple as that.

Remember, Thomas is not called "the twin" for nothing. He has a million siblings, all of whom are perplexed, honorable people. When we feel his doubt, we must do what he did: first, go back to community; second, accept the very human role of a painful pilgrim in search of truth; and, finally, hobnob with people of faith, the folks who, after all their own troubles and doubts, have found a center.

No doubt about it, Thomas is our hero.

The Disguises of Christ

John 10:1–10

The Gardner who spoke softly to the grieving Mary Magdalen in the garden, the Stranger who walked cunningly with the despairing disciples on the road to Emmaus, the Appearance who startled the fearful apostles hiding behind closed doors at the Upper Room, the Cook who appeared on the shore of the lake and prepared fish for incredulous disciples, the Shepherd who pursued with determined love the lost lamb, the Gatekeeper of today's gospel who opens the door to abundant life: we hear all these earthy and descriptive titles used in the gospels of these Sundays after Easter. Gardner, Stranger, Appearance, Cook, Shepherd, Gatekeeper—all these titles, you must realize, are the gospel writers' attempt to convey one truth: Jesus, in many ways and disguises, is alive here and now, and he is active in the everyday-ness of our lives. In other words, Jesus still walks with us, not as a figure from the past but in the present. Jesus is with us, at our side. He is risen. He is alive. He is risen and alive *today*. He is here.

Sometimes, when the moment is just right, we do sense his presence. That is to say, there are encounters in our lives, moments that challenge and change us or give us pause. There are little spiritual revelations that happen to every person. There are times when we feel the closeness of Jesus, hear our name called, and experience our hearts burning within us.

Let me tell you about a woman named Lorraine Murray to whom such an encounter occurred. She is a young married woman who is struggling with breast cancer. She writes articles on the spiritual journey for magazines, and she was encouraged to put them into a book. In the introduction to her book *Grace Notes*, she writes of her sense of Christ's presence:

The[se] essays were born of my desire to know Christ in a more heartfelt way. I longed to dance with Him at a wedding and weep with Him in the garden. I wanted to know the gentle man who loved fishing, eating with His friends, and praying in the desert. I wanted to know the man who invited His friends to a feast He prepared by shouting: "Come and have breakfast...."

[Why not? This was the man who] immersed himself in our broken world. He loved people who were flawed. They were harlots, tax collectors, and thieves. He loved people that others feared, the lepers and the demon-possessed. Instead of shooing away little kids, He hugged them. Instead of condemning His torturers, He forgave them. His love didn't entail big emotional outbursts or passionate proclamations. He loved by serving, by washing His friends' feet and by healing those who were desperate and abandoned. In the 33 years He walked among us, Christ turned the whole world upside down. He told us the poor are rich, the last are first, the meek are blessed, and the dead are alive. Trying to follow His path can seem frustrating—and impossible at times—especially when we feel like we're tripping over every pebble—and boulder—on the way. But, even when we fall into a pit of doubt and sin, He reaches out a hand and lifts us back up.

Lorraine knew all this, felt all this, but one day she let it all go. She continues:

In high school religion classes, the nuns told us about people who were fallen away Catholics, but I never met one until I went to college and became one myself. I fell away from the faith. I turned my back on years of religious training and practice.

The professors had done a good job on her. But living for

herself, having nothing to live by, finding that empty and vain, she eventually came back.

Returning to Catholicism many years later, I discovered something about faith that my childhood catechism hadn't mentioned. Paradoxically enough, the long dry spell of disbelief had produced a robust harvest. I was able to observe the rituals of my religion with fresh eyes and hear the words of Scripture with fresh ears. I was especially thrilled by the story of the Good Shepherd, who was restless and disheartened when even one of His lambs was missing. I pictured myself as a lamb that had wandered far away from Christ for many years and envisioned Christ gently coaxing me to His side. I saw myself nestled against Him as He carried me back to a safe enclosure.

In short, Lorraine again recognized Jesus' voice and followed him. Easter became a reality for her because Easter is the belief in a Jesus who is everything she said. Her story is the same as that of the two disciples on the road to Emmaus or Mary in the garden. And it's our story, too. Even when we're sad and troubled, the Stranger is there. Even when we're in an arid place, the Gardner is there. Even when we're hungry for love and trust, the Cook is there. Even when we're fearful and doubtful, hiding behind closed doors because of our own sins, the Appearance is there. Even when we've strayed and sinned, the Shepherd is there. Even when we feel locked out of life and love, the Gatekeeper is there to let us in to both. Even when we feel him not and our faith is weak; even when we feel all alone, betrayed and abandoned, rejected and hurt, Christ, in some disguise, is at our side

Gardner, Stranger, Cook, Appearance, Gatekeeper, Shepherd: all these descriptions are saying that he is alive now, as we sit here. Jesus is a living presence in our lives, and Easter is the celebration of the Risen Christ who not only daily calls our name as he did to Mary, but calls it with concern and love and promise, as friend to friend. Like the two disciples, we walk with him every day. Like Magdalen, we hear his voice if we but listen.

Like the disciples, we will recognize him if we come out from hiding.

Like sheep in a flock, we gravitate to the One whose voice we recognize because we know that every day he comes to us for one reason only: to open the gate so that we might have life and have it more abundantly.

He Descended into Hell

John 15:1–8

This whole Lent and Easter season has resurrected an old scenario that is embedded deep in the minds of Catholics—at least in minds of the older ones. It goes like this. As a consequence of original sin, the gates of heaven were closed so that, from the time of Adam and Eve until the moment of Jesus' death, nobody could enter paradise. Only a divine act of reparation could give human beings access to heaven. That act of reparation was Jesus' death, which paid the debt of sin and so opened the gates of heaven. Sound familiar?

In this view of things, all the just people who had died from the time of Adam and Eve until Jesus' death were asleep somewhere, in a Hades of sorts or a kind of antechamber. Immediately following his death, Jesus descends to that underworld and awakens these souls, then triumphantly leads them into paradise. That descent is what we understand as "the descent into hell," a phrase we use when we say the Apostles' Creed, not the Nicene Creed we recite at Mass: "He descended into hell and on the third day he rose again."

But I want you to consider descending into hell as an image, something that captures a deeper reality. It's not a videotape of an actual happening; so how, then, is the phrase to be interpreted? How did Jesus descend into hell? What does this mean? I suggest that descending into hell means two things.

For the first meaning, let me offer three images: The first is a story, a tragic one. Some years ago the daughter of a friend of mine committed suicide. She was in her early twenties and away from home when she first attempted to kill herself. The family rushed to her, flew her home, surrounded her with loving solicitude, took her to doctors of every kind, and generally tried every possible way to love and coax her out of her deadly depression. Despite their efforts, she killed herself. Strong as human love can be, sometimes it stands helpless, exhausted, before a door it can't open.

My second image is taken from John's gospel. As John describes it, after Jesus rises from the dead, he appears to the disciples, who are huddled together in fear, in a room with the doors locked. Jesus comes right through the locked doors, stands inside the middle of their fear, and breathes out peace. A week later, he does it again

Here is a third image: when I was a young boy, my mother gave me a holy card, an adaptation of a famous painting by Holman Hunt, "The Christ Who Knocks." In it, we see a man huddled behind a locked door, paralyzed by fear and darkness. Outside the door Jesus stands with a lantern, knocking, ready to relieve the man of his burden. But there's a hitch: the door only has a knob on the inside. Jesus cannot enter unless the man unlocks the door from his side. The implication here is that God cannot help unless we first let God in. Fair enough? Not exactly and here's why.

The cross of Christ reveals that when we are so paralyzed by fear and overcome by darkness that we can no longer help ourselves, God can still come through our locked doors, stand inside our fear and paralysis, and breathe out peace. The love that is revealed in Jesus' suffering and death is so other-centered that it can forgive and embrace its executioners, pass through locked doors, melt frozen hearts, and penetrate the walls of fear. In a word, it can descend into our private hells and breathe peace.

There it is; there is the key. "He descended into hell" means that there is no hell where Jesus cannot, will not, be. They haven't yet invented the hell where his love cannot penetrate.

They haven't yet built the door that his love cannot pass through. That's what the phrase means. The young woman who committed suicide had reached a point where she was frozen inside a private hell, behind doors that her family's love and professional doctors could no longer open. I have no doubt that when she awoke on the other side, she found Christ standing inside her fear and darkness, breathing out peace. "He descended into hell" means that Jesus' love is there in the worst places of our lives.

As disciples of Jesus, we too must descend into hell. Let me illustrate by sharing a story about that wonderful man, Pope John XXIII, now Blessed Pope John.

Shortly after he was elected pope, he visited the Regina Coeli prison outside Rome, setting off an international orgy of press reporting. There he is on film, a confident, cheerful old man, his soft brown eyes alight, completely at ease with himself and his audience, gesturing expressively with his big farmer's hands and speaking with spontaneity, obviously making up his comments as he goes along. He tells the prisoners that, since they couldn't come to see him, he came to see them.

The Pope said that he came from poor people. Then he added, "There are only three ways of losing money in Italy: farming, gambling, and women. My father chose the least interesting way." He told them that one of his brothers had been caught poaching; an uncle had done time. "These are the things that happen to poor people," he said, and then added, "But we are all children of God. And I; I am your brother." The audience—from priests to politicians, from convicts to jailers—wept openly. In the film you can see copious tears coursing down hardened faces.

Suddenly, a murderer dared approach the pope to ask: "Can there be forgiveness for me?" In answer, the Pope just took the murderer in his arms and hugged him, heedless of all danger to his person, let alone to his dignity. John was truly a pope such as the world had never seen, a pope who descended into hell, who went into a prison to release those awaiting salvation.

Pope John even went into the hell of atheism when he received Nikita Khrushchev's daughter, Rada, and her husband, Alexis. When they came into the room, the Pope heard Rada Khrushchev whisper to her husband, in Russian, to look closely at the Pope's hands, which she described as "the beautiful hands of a Russian peasant." She did not know that her host understood her native language, and the Pope was deeply moved by her words.

The Pope then asked Rada to tell him the names of her children, not because he didn't already know them (he did), but "because when a mother speaks the names of her children, something exceptional happens," he said. He then asked her to caress her children for him, especially the one named Ivan (Russian for John). As his gift, John gave her, the atheist, a rosary, saying he knew she wouldn't wish to use it, but he wanted her to have it nonetheless "because it reminds me of peace in the home, and of my mother, who used to say it by the fireside when I was a child," said the Pope. Then he asked the couple to accept his blessing, not the blessing of a pope—which he knew they, as official atheists, could not accept—just the blessing of an old man. They left smiling and in tears; to this day Rada has kept the rosary and calls it "one of my most precious possessions." That's the kind of man Pope John was. Like Jesus, he descended into hell.

The Easter season is nearly over, and Pentecost is at our doorsteps. As renewed Christians, this the time when we open our lives for the descent of Jesus, knowing that whatever private hell we harbor, it will not keep him from coming into our lives. Also, it is a time when we who follow Jesus visit others' private hells to offer them kindness, compassion, love, and a hug.

You see how powerful and meaningful is that mysterious phrase, "He descended into hell." What reassurance this is to take with us as we journey. What an example to follow as an Easter people.

Ordinary Time

I Came to You in Weakness

1 Corinthians 2:1–5

"I came to you in weakness and in fear and in much trembling."
Weren't these St. Paul's words in today's second reading? Yes: "I came to you in weakness." He went on to say, you recall, "My speech and my proclamation were not with plausible words of wisdom...." So what did he offer? "A demonstration of the Spirit and of power."

Paul is right, and he speaks for all of us. That's probably the best anyone here has to offer: some talent, some intelligence, some ability. In the end, however, whatever the rich variety or lack of what we have to offer, we all have one common gift: our weaknesses. At best we are all flawed, and, on the brink of Lent, we reluctantly and collectively and publicly admit it. It is a rare occasion, indeed, but there it is: we admit it, out loud. We have our weaknesses but—and here is the message of today's Scripture—we are to witness from that weakness.

No excuses allowed. None of this "I am not worthy" stuff. Who here is worthy? No protestations that I am not gifted or powerful or capable, for that is just the point Paul is making. He would say that, from the very depths of such weakness, we must do what we can to make this world a moral and decent place to live in. The little we have is enough. God will do the rest.

Well, these are lofty, powerful, and very true thoughts. As is my wont, however, I must move them around, rearrange them, and finally, translate them with a story, so we all understand what Paul was saying. My story, a true story, goes like this. On November 18, 1995, Itzhak Perlman, the violinist, came on stage to give a concert at Lincoln Center in New York City. Now, if you have ever been to a Perlman concert, you know that getting on stage is no small achievement for him. Because he was stricken with polio as a child, he has braces on both legs and walks with the aid of two crutches.

To see him walk slowly across the stage, one step at a time, is a sight. He walks painfully, yet majestically, until he reaches his chair. He sits down slowly, puts his crutches on the floor, undoes the clasps on his legs, tucks one foot back, and extends the other foot forward. Then he bends down and picks up the violin, puts it under his chin, nods to the conductor, and proceeds to play. By now, the audience is used to this ritual. They sit quietly while he makes his way across the stage to his chair. They remain reverently silent while he undoes the clasps on his legs. They wait until he is ready to play.

But on this particular night, something went wrong. Just as Perlman finished the first few bars, one of the strings on his violin broke. You could hear it snap. It went off like gunfire across the room. There was no mistaking what that sound meant; there was no mistaking what he had to do. People thought that he would have to get up, put on his clasps again, pick up the crutches, and limp his way offstage either to find another violin or to find another string for this one. Or, he would have to wait for someone to bring him another.

But he didn't. Instead, Perlman waited a moment, closed his eyes, and then signaled the conductor to begin again. The orchestra began, and he played from where he had left off. And he played with a passion and a power and a purity such as they had never heard before. Of course, everyone knows that it is impossible to play a symphonic work with just three strings. I know that and you know that, but that night Itzhak Perlman refused to know it. You could see him modulating, changing, recomposing the piece in his head. At one point, it sounded like he was de-tuning the strings to get new sounds from them, sounds they had never made before.

When he finished, there was an awesome silence in the room. And then people rose and cheered. There was an extraordinary outburst of applause from every corner of the auditorium. Everyone was on their feet, screaming and cheering, doing everything they could to show how much they appreciated what he had done. Perlman smiled, wiped the sweat from his brow, raised his bow to quiet the people, and then he said, not boastfully, but in a quiet, pensive, reverent tone: "You know, sometimes it is the artist's task to find out how much music you can still make with what you have left."

What a powerful line that is. It has stayed in my mind ever since I heard it. And who knows? Perhaps that is the way of life, not just for an artist but for all of us. Here is a man who has prepared all his life to make music on a violin with four strings, who all of a sudden, in the middle of a concert, finds himself with only three strings. And the music he made that night with just three strings was more beautiful, more sacred, more memorable than any that he had ever made before, when he had four strings.

So, perhaps there is our message and what St. Paul meant: our task in this shaky, fast-changing, bewildering world in which we live is to make music—at first with all that we have, and then, when that is no longer possible, to make music with what we have left. Looking at Itzhak Perlman, Lent is a good time to take inventory on how we have used our gifts, however meager and flawed. We may be sick, elderly, poor, depressed, betrayed, wronged, slow, impaired, grieving, or sinful; in short, we may be stuck with three strings. But the challenge is to do good with what we have left. If we have squandered our three-stringed gifts, we have sinned and must repent. If we have become closed in on ourselves, we must resolve this Lent to be open to the needs of others. It's as simple as that.

So I bring up Itzahk Perlman because even with his crutches

and braces and his broken string, he delights us. Closer to home I think of a close friend of mine who just celebrated twenty-six years of sobriety. All these years she has come, in her weakness, to counsel and sit with alcoholics and drug addicts to coax them out of their imprisonment. I'm thinking of the blind nun in South Jersey who has turned out to be a wonderful spiritual director. I think of Renoir painting masterpieces with arthritic hands. I think of those parents who have lost children and who started Compassionate Friends for others who have felt that keen loss.

The point is, we can all make music with what we have, and with what we have left. True enough, we may all be like St. Paul in weakness, but we are still challenged to demonstrate the Spirit. Lent is a good time for us three-string people to start.

Ordinary Time

Mark 1:29–39

A cabby picks up a nun. She gets into the cab, and the cab driver won't stop staring at her. She asks him why is he staring, and he replies, "I have a question to ask you, but I don't want to offend you." She answers, "My dear son, you cannot offend me. When you're as old as I am and have been a nun as long as I have, you get a chance to see and hear just about everything. I'm sure that there's nothing you could say or ask that I would find offensive."

"Well," he says, "I've always had a fantasy to have a nun kiss me."

She responds, "Let's see what we can do about that. Number 1, you have to be single and number 2, you must be Catholic."

The cab driver becomes very excited and says, "Yes, yes, I'm single, and I'm Catholic too."

"OK," the nun says, "pull over to the side."

He does, and the nun fulfills his fantasy with a quick peck on the cheek. But when they get back on the road, the cab driver starts crying.

"My dear child," said the nun, "why are you crying?"

"Forgive me sister, but I have sinned. I lied. I must confess, I'm married, and I'm Jewish."

The nun says, "That's OK, my name is Kevin, and I'm on my way to a Halloween party."

The trouble with telling a funny story like that is that you'll remember it and not what I'm setting you up for.

Listen carefully, so that when you remember the joke you may also remember its point. As many of you know, the liturgical or church year revolves around the life of Jesus. So, we began our year with Advent, then we moved into Christmas, Epiphany, and the Baptism of Jesus. The next big focus on Jesus will be at Lent and Easter and Pentecost.

But right now, we're in the in-between time, known as Ordinary Time, and today is the Fifth Sunday in Ordinary Time. But Ordinary Time doesn't mean unimportant. Ordinary Time means daily living-out the themes of the extraordinary times. It's like the afterglow of the birthday party or anniversary or graduation, which says, "now let's get back to everyday life."

But getting back to everyday life doesn't mean dullness and boredom. It means discovering God in the everyday-ness of life or uncovering the religious dimensions of everyday life. This is to say that God is present in and through the ordinary things of the world, that ordinary things can be revelations of the divine.

Let me explain by referring to a high school teacher, who writes that young people sometimes have a difficult time seeing how the sacred relates to their ordinary experience. He says that for many, the realm of the holy lies beyond their everyday, conscious horizon. The holy, the young people say (as do many adults), can only be experienced inside a church building, as something descending "from above" but with little to say to the rest of the week.

This teacher recently read with his students the poem entitled "High Flight," written by John Gillespie Macgee, Jr., not long before he was shot down in battle. Macgee, a fighter pilot in World War II, describes in the poem how flying helped him "touch the face of God." So the teacher asked his students to reflect on an activity that has allowed them to touch the face of God. He shares some samples of what they wrote:

The things that make me feel as if I could touch the face of God are times when I am overwhelmed by love and friendship. The last time I went to a family reunion, I was touched by the level of loving and caring everyone showed me.

There's nothing like the feeling of being loved. I would say that love is the one thing in life that can truly take a person to another level in life, because the source behind love and the source behind just about everything is God.

Another student wrote:

In my life, I think that the only activity that helps me touch the face of God is probably listening to or making music. When I listen to music, I am amazed at the ability that musicians have to make such wonderful sound. The creativity, in many ways, is "mind-blowing," and it makes the experience totally beautiful.

In another assignment the students were asked to reflect on their own experiences of wonder and awe, whereby they recognize their own smallness in relation to a mystery that goes totally beyond themselves. One student wrote:

During the summer I actually set up a tent in my backyard. It may sound odd, but there is some allure to distancing myself from technology and returning to an old way of life. It's nice just to lay down, hear the birds chirp, smell freshly cut grass, and look up to see the blue sky through open tent flaps. We take a lot of things for granted, the chirp of birds, the meandering scuttle of ants, the chirp of crickets, everything that God has created.

Another student describes his awe-filled experience of the Mississippi River:

There is a park on the river I can ride my bike to. A couple of years ago, my brother took me there for the first time on bikes. We first rode through the park and then through the woods. Eventually, we reached the river. We got off our bikes and walked right up to the Mississippi River. There I was standing with my brother, this huge river splashing at our feet. I looked out at the water splashing every which way. So far distant across the river was Illinois. I knew God was there. The place was amazing. It immediately struck me as one of those times in which silence seems the only adequate response to greatness.

These students were articulating what is called the experience of transcendence—the signal that there's more to life than what appears on the surface—in the midst of the ordinary, natural settings of everyday life. By giving time to these moments of depth and transcendence, they were discovering the religious elements of their own everyday experience.

And that's my message; that's what Ordinary Time is all about. God is present in the routine of life, in ordinary things and people, if we but notice. In the joke I told earlier, behind the single Catholic cabbie was a married Jewish driver. Behind the pious nun was a kid having fun. Behind what we see everyday, the people and the realities, is a Presence, a caring God, a transcendent love. Ordinary Time is an opportunity to sense that. Let me end with a poem I had to learn as a kid in school. It says in a nutshell everything those students were saying:

I see his blood upon the rose
And in the stars the glory of his eyes,
His body gleams amid eternal snows,
His tears fall from the skies.

I see his face in every flower,
The thunder and the singing of the birds
Are but his voice—and carven by his power
Rocks are his written words.

All pathways by his feet are worn.
His strong heart stirs the ever-beating sea,
His crown of thorns is twined with every thorn,
His cross is every tree.

Roses, stars, snow, sky, flower, thunder, birds, rocks, pathways, sea, thorns, tree—all are ordinary. All are revelation.

Unable to Get Near Jesus

Mark 2:1–12

This is a colorful gospel. It has that "made-for-television" quality about it: a crowded doorway, a clever idea, surprising everyone by lowering your friend through the hole in the roof, the verbal exchanges, and so on. Everyone, I suspect, has his or her favorite mental image of this scene. I have mine. In fact, I have a favorite phrase in the story that has always captivated me because it's so evocative, so rich. It comes at the very beginning of the story, and it's about the sick man and his four friends. The words are "…unable to get near Jesus because of the crowd."

How about that? "Unable to get near Jesus because of the crowd." Immediately I think of certain people, of how that line is a perfect take on them. You know, the people who can't get near Jesus because there's something, someone, blocking the way. Offhand, three categories of people spring to mind here: the backward-lookers, the defeated, and the addicted. I have a story for each one of these.

The first one is in the form of a little allegory and it's titled "The City of Regret." It goes like this:

I had not really planned to take a trip this year, yet I found myself packing anyway. And off I went, dreading it. I was on another guilt trip. I booked my reservation on Wish I Had airlines. I didn't check my bags—everyone carries their bag-

91

gage on this airline. I had to drag my bags for what seemed like miles in the Regret City airport. And I could see that people from all over the world were there with me, limping along under the weight of bags they had packed themselves. I caught a cab to Last Resort Hotel, the driver taking the whole trip backward, looking over his shoulder. And there I found the ballroom where my event would be held: the Annual Pity Party. As I checked in, I saw that all my old colleagues were on the guest list: The Done family—Woulda, Coulda and Shoulda; both of the members of the Opportunity family were there—Missed and Lost. All the Yesterdays were there, too; there were too many to count, but all would have sad stories to share. Shattered Dreams and Broken Promises would be there, too, along with their friends Don't Blame Me and I Couldn't Help It. And of course, hours and hours of entertainment would be provided by that renowned storyteller, It's Their Fault. As I prepared to settle in for a really long night, I realized that one person had the power to send all those people home and break up the party: me. All I had to do was, with some help, return to the present and welcome the new day!

There it is. All those people burdened with guilt from the past, always looking over their shoulders, always rehearsing what might have been, should have been, would have been, always licking old wounds like a divorce, a betrayal, a disappointment, an unfairness—that's a lot of people blocking the way. No wonder they are unable to to get near Jesus.

After the backward lookers comes the second category: the defeated, those who are defeated by life's blows and hurts and rotten deals. My story here is one you may already know, the story of retail genius, J.C. Penney. In the early years of the Great Depression, Penney lost a large part of his fortune, the fruit of thirty years of hard work, and he suffered a nervous breakdown. In the hospital, which he could ill afford, the fifty-eight-year-old businessman confronted his deepest fears and questioned his most dearly held values. He later described his turning point:

One night, I became possessed of the strange idea that the end of life had come for me and that before morning I would be gone. I took a sedative, and I went to sleep at nine o'clock. After an hour I awoke, still with the conviction that this was the last night on earth for me. I got up, wrote farewell letters to my family, returned to bed, and again fell asleep. To my surprise I was still alive the following morning. Feeling restless and apprehensive, I dressed and went downstairs to the dining room, intending to have breakfast. The place had not yet been opened. I wandered disconsolate down the corridor. Presently the sound of singing led me to the chapel where a small group of people were engaged in an early morning prayer meeting. They were singing the old, familiar hymn, "Be not dismayed whate'er betide, God will take care of you."

Slipping inside, I sat down in one of the back seats. Someone read a passage of Scripture which was followed by a prayer. Silently, yet in agony of spirit, I cried: "Lord, I can do nothing! Will *you* take care of me?" Something I can only explain as a miracle happened to me. In that quiet chapel an appalling weight was lifted from my spirit, and I passed from darkness to light. I had entered the room paralyzed in spirit and helplessly adrift. I left it with an exhilarating sense of relief from the thought of impending death and a reborn hope in life.

We'll come back to J.C. Penney.

Finally, the addicted are really unable to get near Jesus. Listen to this man.

My drug use began to destroy my family relationships. I remember one day that I had promised my son that I would pick him up on payday, and we would spend the day together. Instead of using my check for a day with him, I stopped and bought some stuff and got high. This happened right around the corner from his house, but I never made it there because getting high had become more important. Another day I even caused my own mother to pull a gun on me because I wanted some money back that

I had given her to keep for me. She told me that she would rather kill me than see me living like I was!

The drugs had such a grip on me that I still went out and got high. Upon returning to my room, I sat on my bed and decided that Mom was right, that it would be better to die than live this life. I toyed with my mother's gun, and as I sat there looking at it, the alarm clock beside my bed suddenly went off. I truly believe that this was nothing short of an act of God, getting my attention. As I reached for the alarm, I slowly pushed the gun aside. I realized that today was my son's birthday! I didn't want him to have to live his life remembering this day as the day his dad died.

Seeking help, I entered a hospital in Philadelphia. While lying in my bed, I heard a nurse telling another man about a program in Harrisburg, Pennsylvania that had changed her brother's life. The man she was talking to was not interested in hearing what she had to say, but God touched my heart right then and right there. God used this nurse to save my life. After talking with her, I got on a train to Harrisburg.

Now, over three years later, I am truly free. It was the Christ-centered program of Bethesda that the Lord used to release me from the shackles of fear and doubt that had kept me in bondage for so long.

These and others can't get near Jesus: their phobias, fears, defeats, sins, and guilt are in the way. But they, like the man in the gospel, all had one common thing in their favor that redeemed them—and here is where you come into this gospel: they had friends.

The four friends in the gospel circumvented the crowd and brought their good friend to Jesus. The man from the City of Regret said that, with the help of a good friend, he could look to a future of love rather than a past of regret. J.C. Penney's "four friends" were a bunch of folks praying and singing in the early morning. The addicted man's friend was a nurse who cared not only for his body, but also for his soul.

You see where this gospel is leading, don't you? There is someone out there whom you must help to bypass the crowd—

those ghostly shades of regret, guilt, and despair—and bring them to Jesus, because the fact is that they won't get there without you. Or, to put it simply, everyone here, by virtue of his or her baptism, by virtue of being a Christian, is a designated friend.

Calling All Matthews

Matthew 9:9–13

"As he sat at dinner in the house, many tax collectors and sinners came and were sitting with Jesus and his disciples."

I love imagining that scene. Can't you see it in your mind's eye? Try. Jesus saw a fellow Jew named Matthew collecting taxes for the Roman occupiers. Matthew was a despicable man by any terms, disdained by the Romans and hated by the Jews. He was a schemer, a quisling, a cheat. Yet Jesus called him. Talk about scandal in the Church—then more scandal. Matthew, with his ill-gotten money, throws a dinner party. That was bad enough, but there was a final scandal: the guests turned out to be as bad as Matthew himself, tax collectors and sinners, and they ate with Jesus. Can you image what that room looked like with a guest list like that, a bunch of cutthroats and low-lifes eating with Jesus? As one scholar put it:

> In societies where there are barriers between classes, races, or other status groups, the separation is maintained by means of a taboo on social mixing. You do not share a meal or a dinner party, you do not celebrate or participate in entertainment with people who belong to another social group. In the Middle East sharing a meal at table with someone is a particularly intimate form of association and friendship. They would never, even out of politeness, eat or drink with a person of a lower class or status, or with any person of whom they disapproved.

And yet here was Jesus, saying that for him barriers between people do not exist. In fact, he had a habit of disregarding barriers and would demonstrate it over and over again as he touched an untouchable leper, healed a gentile's servant, cured a foreign woman's daughter, and mischievously told the story of the socially bad Samaritan who was morally good.

Anyway, looking around at that crowd eating with Jesus leaves no doubt about the message. There are no barriers with Jesus Christ. No one is excluded from the love of God, no matter how bad they are or have been. All the Matthews down through the ages are welcomed to the banquet if they but get up immediately and follow him even at the last minute.

Toward the end of Eugene O'Neill's wonderful play, *The Great God Brown*, a man named Billy is on his deathbed, and he's very frightened. At his side is a woman who has become something of a mother figure to him in these last moments of his life. So she speaks to him as though he were a child, saying, "Go to sleep, Billy. It's all right." And he says, "Yes, mother."

Then he starts to explain what he has experienced in life. "It was dark," he says, "and I couldn't see where I was going, and they all picked on me." The woman says, "I know. But you're tired now. Go to sleep." He asks, "And when I wake up?" She replies, "The sun will be rising." Then Billy interrupts and says, in great seriousness, "To judge the living and the dead." Then, in great fear, he adds, "I don't want justice; I want love." The woman replies quietly, "There is only love." And as he dies, Billy begins to repeat the words of the only prayer he knows: "Our Father who art in heaven...." For sinners like Billy and Matthew, there is only love, at least according to Jesus who broke bread with them.

I remember my own version of Matthew. It was a woman named Maria. Seeing the ad the church had put in the paper for a secretary, she had made an appointment with me for an interview. Much to my chagrin I soon found out that she had another agenda in mind because as soon as she entered my office, Maria let loose on me.

A former Catholic, as it turned out, Maria was currently the secretary to a very bigoted anti-Catholic fundamentalist group, and before I could even begin to explain the job to her, she proceeded to denounced everything having to do with me, God, or the Church. Her bitterness startled and overwhelmed me. Trying to recover my composure, I tried to listen respectfully and reply gently to everything Maria said.

Soon, Maria was telling me her life story. It was a tale of pain and suffering and sin—lots of sin. She ended each diatribe with one question, "Supposing there is a God, would he accept a woman like me?" I did not hesitate to answer her for I just happened to be preparing my homily precisely on today's gospel, and so I had ready at hand its last verse: "For I have come to call not the righteous but sinners." I repeated that to Maria, but she ignored me and tried to explain once again all the sins she had recently committed. I countered with Matthew's words: "I have come to call not the righteous but sinners."

No less than seventeen times Maria tried to explain to me why she was unworthy to receive forgiveness. Seventeen times, I simply repeated the words, "I have come to call not the righteous but sinners." I don't know if I wore her down, but finally, Maria bowed her head, cried a little and asked me, "Would you hear my confession? I want to come home." She didn't get the job, which she really didn't want, but like Matthew, she got what she really *did* want: forgiveness, peace, and a return to her true home. And there she was in my mind's eye: at the table with Matthew, Billy, the tax collectors, sinners—and Jesus.

The spiritual writer Henri Nouwen, in search of his own healing from an overextended schedule, went to Peru to work among the poor. He lived in a slum, and the family he stayed with had few possessions. Yet Nouwen felt their love through the children who crawled all over him, giggling, squirming, and playing games with the strange priest who spoke their language like a child. He wrote:

How little do we really know of the power of physical touch. These boys and girls only wanted one thing: to be touched, hugged, stroked, and caressed. Probably most adults have the same need but no longer have the innocence and unself-consciousness to express them. Sometimes I see humanity as a sea of people starving for affection, tenderness, care, love, acceptance, forgiveness.... Everyone seems to cry, "Please, love me."

The gospel story of Matthew says that there stands Jesus ready to do so. As Mother Teresa said of the lepers she treated, "We have drugs for people with diseases like leprosy, but these drugs do not treat the main problem, the disease of being unwanted." And there stands Jesus who *does* want us, disease and all.

There is no question but that the Matthew story is our story. Like Matthew, we find ourselves at this banquet of the Mass with Jesus and the rest of the outcasts and sinners who fill this church today. At Communion time, as you reach out and embrace the gift of bread, do so with the humility and gratitude that Matthew must have felt. Rejoice that Jesus has said, "I did not come to call the righteous but sinners," and that at this Mass we have answered the invitation to be transformed, like Matthew, from sinner to apostle.

The Month of June

Matthew 9:36–10:8

There is, I must confess up front, nothing exciting or especially thrilling in what I am about to share, so you can listen half-heartedly and even catch a nap.

The calling of the twelve apostles was really quite ordinary, if you think about it. Hardly anybody even knew about it back then. Even more, these apostles themselves were so ordinary that most of us can't name all of them. We know next to nothing about them, who they were and what happened to them after Jesus' ascension. And so, seeing how seemingly minor and unimportant their choosing was, yet knowing what an impact it had on us here today, I wanted to reflect on some ordinary people who have similarly touched our lives deeply during this ordinary and lovely month of June.

First, the name of the month itself: June. It comes from the Latin word *juriores*, meaning "young," because this is a time of joy for the young: school's out, they get married. School bells silenced and wedding bells chiming are signs of youth's joy. The name also refers to the Roman goddess Juno, who was the patron of Roman women from birth to death. Whatever way you look at it, the motif of June is joy.

Let's take a look at some of the notable events that have occurred in June.

On June 1, 1619, the first Negro slaves arrived in Virginia. Who would have thought that our country would be founded on slavery, and that the seeds of prejudice and the civil rights movement were planted here, along with cotton? Rosa Parks, Martin Luther King, Jr., George Wallace, Malcolm X, Robert Kennedy, Jr.—their spirits still hover. What an impact this seemingly unimportant event has had, even to this very day.

June 4: besides being a date world-famous for my ordination in 1955, on this date in 1896 at 2:00 AM, the first Ford rolled off the assembly line. If you don't think that has had an impact on the world, think of it as you get in your cars after Mass, jockey to exit the parking lot first, fighting the summertime traffic!

June 7 marks the death of the prophet Mohammed in 632 AD. Think about the impact of Islam on the world since that time (remember the Crusades?), certainly up to this very day.

On June 10, 1935, Dr. Paul Smith and Bill Wilson founded Alcoholics Anonymous. Their famous twelve steps have saved the lives of many an alcoholic. Who would have thought that two people could make such a difference to so many addicted people, to society?

June 15, 1215: the Magna Carta was signed by King John on this day, and the beginning of democracy, including our bill of rights, was set in motion.

Today is Father's Day. When a group of children was asked "What does love mean?" Billy, age four, declared that "When someone loves you, the way they say your name is different." I love that. Terri, also four, answered, "Love is what makes you smile when you're tired." Eight-year-old Cindy said, "When I was on stage and scared, I looked at all the people watching me and saw my daddy, waving and smiling. He was the only one doing that. I wasn't scared anymore." Fathers are like that. Their impact is immeasurable; their absence is devastating.

June 25, 1876 was the day of Custer's last stand, his defeat by Chiefs Sitting Bull and Crazy Horse near the Little Big Horn river in Montana.

June 27, 1880 saw the birth of one of the most truly remarkable women of all times: Helen Keller.

Then there are religious events commemorated in June that have changed our lives. June 5 marks the feast of St. Boniface, the patron saint of Germany and beer brewers. He and other missionaries like him brought the faith to Europe. June 24 is the feast day of John the Baptist, the outspoken prophet who was the cousin of Jesus. June 29 is the feast of our two founding apostles, Peter and Paul. And, of course, the entire month of June is dedicated to the Sacred Heart of Jesus.

So, there we are: the month of June. Slavery, assembly-line automobiles, Islam, the Magna Carta, June weddings, school endings, St. Boniface, Bill Wilson, John the Baptist, Peter, Paul, Custer, Helen Keller: all in the same month. All these events and all these real people—not the manufactured, passing celebrity creations of today—unknown and unheralded at the time, insignificant and unnoticed, a bit part on the world's stage, a splinter floating on the ocean of time, a speck in the cosmos. Yet how they have affected our lives!

Jesus summoned his disciples. We don't know where; we don't know when. We do have twelve names, four or five of whom we really know anything about. Jesus gave them all power, and he gave them all a mission. And look how these unknowns have affected our lives.

I don't know about you, but I like to come to church to hear a homily that will get me through the week. So, is there a lesson here for us to take home as we contemplate the month of June, the month of joy, and those who people it? Yes. It is this: we, who are also unknown and unheralded in our time, have been summoned every bit as those twelve apostles. Like them, we have been given power and a mission by our baptism.

Every Mass, therefore, is a reaffirmation of our importance, our identity, and our mission. Every Mass reminds us of our dignity as children of God. Every Mass tells us that we should be June-children, children of joy, because we have received the Good News and are designated to *be* the good news.

Every Mass challenges us: what can we do this coming week to make this world better, to be better Christians? Every Mass asks: what will future generations say of us? How will we have blessed them, whether they know our name or not?

What will we take home today? Nothing more and nothing less than the truism that we too have been called, that our name is on the calendar. Make it count for Jesus.

Life's Burdens

Matthew 11:25–30

Sooner or later most of us wake up to the sense that the life we are living is not exactly the life we hoped it might be. We realize that life has its burdens, three of which are prominent.

The first is the burden of daily irritations: you know, standing in line at the Post Office or at the Department of Motor Vehicles; forced to listen to gangsta rap while on hold for a half hour; trying to figure out tax forms or the endless legalisms of Medicare, HMOs, and the IRS. The frictions and irritations of daily life are a burden we all bear.

The second burden includes the more serious stuff of life: poverty, illness, loss, the pain of an unhealed marriage, the fear of family violence, the endless expectations others impose on us, trusted institutions, like some corporations or the Church, that fail to be compassionate and sometimes betray our trust. Then there are the hurts that don't heal, anger that won't go away, success that's always just beyond our reach. We can be a burden to others; and they, to us.

The third burden we carry is deepest of all, although not always obvious as we tend to suppress it. This is the burden of identity: who am I, really? What core remains when all the shifting sands of time empty out? Beneath the cosmetics, the facade, the tyranny of fashion and wannabees, who am I? All during our lives we try to answer that question.

The first answer we often come up with, because the culture tells us so, is "I am what I do." In its own way, this is very true.

When I do good things and have a little success in life, I feel good about myself. But when I fail or get old or sick or down-sized and can't do what I used to do, I start feeling low or depressed and wonder, now that I am no longer what I did, who am I?

Or we might say, "I am what other people say about me." This is a very powerful thought; in fact, it is sometimes most important. When people speak well of you, you can walk around quite freely. But when somebody starts saying negative things about you, you might start feeling sad and having doubts about yourself. You might try on other false identities hoping to please others and reclaim their favorable comments. But by so doing, you forfeit your true identity.

Finally, you might also say, "I am what I have." For example, I am an American with kind parents, a good education, good health, and tons of clothes, furniture, and cars. But as soon as I lose any of it, if a family member dies or my health goes or I lose the property I have, then I can slip into inner darkness and feel I am nobody. And, in fact, if I lose all I have, I become an unnoticed has-been with no face, and the society which once idolized me evaporates.

Nevertheless, we put a lot of energy into maintaining our beliefs that "I am what I do," "I am what others say about me," "I am what I have." And you know, when that's the case, our life quickly becomes a repetitive up and down motion. Because when people speak well about us, and when we do good things and have a lot, we are quite "up" and excited. But when we start losing, when suddenly we find out that we can't do anything anymore, when we find out that people are talking against us, when we lose our friends, we might slip into depression, feel very low, and become something of non-persons.

And before you realize it, we are on a zigzag, up and down, up and down. That's why most of our work and our mental energy goes toward trying to stay above the line, and we call that surviving. We want to hold on to our good name, hold on to some good work, hold on to our property; but we know that in the end there is the reality that says we are going to die after all. We're going to lose it all. You know, when you live this kind of life, with all these ups and downs, the end is death. And when you are dead, you're dead. Nobody talks about you anymore; you don't have anything anymore; you can't do anything anymore. You lose it all. That little life of yours and mine has come to nothing. And that means we are nothing.

What I want to say to you today is that this whole thing is wrong. That is not who you are, and it is not who I am. That is what the demon said to Jesus when he went to the desert: "Turn the stones into bread, and show the world that you can do something." "Jump from the temple, and let people catch you, so they speak well of you." "Kneel in front of me, and I will give you a lot of possessions. Then you will be loved by everybody, and you will know who you are." But Jesus says, "That is a lie. I already know who I am because before the Spirit sent me to be tempted by you, the Spirit came upon me and said to me, "You are the beloved Child. You are my beloved Son. On you my favor rests."

This truth was the basic identity that Jesus clung to as he lived his life with its ups and downs. People praised him, and people rejected him, and people said, "Hosanna," and people said, "Crucify him." It made no difference; Jesus held on to the core truth. "Whatever happens, I am the beloved of God, and that is who I am and will always be. That truth allows me to live in a world that keeps rejecting me or praising me or laughing at me or spitting on me. I am the beloved. Not because people say I'm great, but because my Father says so. He has forever called me Beloved."

Dear friends, if there is anything that I want you to hear this morning, it is that what is said of Jesus is also said of you: you are the beloved daughter or son of God. That is your core identity. And you must hear this truth not only in your head but in your gut, hear it so that your whole life can be turned around. You must cling to the truth, the joy, the conviction that you are the beloved sons and daughters of God before, during, and after all the burdens of life. That is the one unchangeable reality in your lives. Therefore, every time that you are tempted to despair, become bitter or jealous, or lash out; every time you feel rejected—in fact, *are* rejected—or laughed at or made fun of or passed over, say, "No matter what happens to me, I am the beloved son the beloved daughter of God."

Remember this story? The line at the airport was long, the crowd pressing. The man at the head of the line was furious: "I want to be seated now! I can't wait in this line. I've got first-class tickets," he screamed. He went on and on. The attendant behind the counter was patiently trying to explain the problems to him, but he would have none of it. Finally he shouted, "Do you know who I am?" Immediately, the sharp-witted attendant picked up the microphone and announced: "Attention, we have a gentleman here who doesn't know who he is. If anyone can identify this man, please come to the front desk."

We laugh and take pleasure in his comeuppance; but here is a man who has all his identity wrapped up in what he does, what people say about him, and what he possesses. When these are threatened, he cries out in pain, for what is left when this material identity is challenged or gone?

What is left, if he but knew it, is that he is Beloved.

Biblical Saints

Romans 8:26–27

Likewise the Spirit helps us in our weakness. That very Spirit intercedes with sighs too deep for words....The Spirit intercedes for the saints according to the will of God.

So writes St. Paul in today's second reading. I want to reflect on his use of the word "saint," because it did not mean the same thing to Paul as it does to us. To us, a saint is someone who has been canonized, someone who has led a virtuous life. For Paul and his Jewish ancestors, saint meant something entirely different. For them, a saint wasn't someone who necessarily led a virtuous life, but someone who, however unvirtuous, was suddenly called by God and, perhaps even to their own surprise, responded.

That's why, to use a racy example, Scripture can refer to a prostitute as a saint. Why? Because of her faith in the God who called and to whom she responded. Let me fill you in on this Old Testament story, which reads like a TV script: Joshua, Moses' successor, has led the army of Israel to the threshold of the promised land. Then spies are sent to reconnoiter Jericho. As soldiers often do, they end up at Rahab's place in a seedy section of town. (Rahab is the prostitute I mentioned before.) Somehow, the king received word that spies were about, so he sent his police to seize them. When the police inquired at Rahab's house, she lied. Batting her heavy eyelashes, she said, "True, a couple of Hebrew boys were here earlier, but when the gate was closed at dark, they left; go quickly and maybe you'll overtake them."

The king's men rushed on, not knowing that Madame Rahab had hidden the Israelites on her roof. Had they been found, it would have cost her her life. She knew that, but she did it anyway. Why did she hide them? Because, she told the spies, she had heard of the mighty works of their God, and so all she asks is that the Israelites show her family mercy when the walls of Jericho come tumbling down. Then, while it was still night, Rahab let them down by a rope, and he tied a scarlet thread in her window to identify her place for the invading Israelites.

When Joshua and his army finally entered the city, the folk of the red thread house in the red light district were the only ones spared when the invaders leveled Jericho. Today, Rahab is a heroine and celebrated.

But it gives us pause. A prostitute. A liar. What kind of saint is that? What's worse, she's not alone. Drunken, naked Noah, Abraham and his squabbling family, old mean-spirited, conniving Sarah, murderer Moses, lustful David, bigoted Paul: we would label them all unholy. Yet the Bible honors them as saints. If that puzzles you—and it should—remember that the Bible simply has a different notion of sainthood than we do. As I said before, a biblical saint is not a person who has been virtuous throughout his or her life. No, biblical saintliness is a matter of what God does with people and how they respond.

In the Bible, a person is regarded as a saint because God wants that person to do something holy, *not* because that person *is* holy. Biblical saints are those who are called to do God's work, no matter how unworthy or shady they are, and who accept the call. Sainthood in the Bible means being commandeered by God, no matter how wicked you are, and doing what God wants. In short, biblical saints are those who listen to God and who say "yes"—at least for this one, critical time—regardless of the mess they are and the risk they have to take. It's their moment of grace, as it were, and they take it. And all is redeemed.

I kind of like that definition better than ours, which insists on continuous, wondrous virtue and nobility in its saints. In the Bible, an evil person can claim sainthood by accepting a noble deed, regardless of the cost. Oskar Schindler, by all accounts a despicable man, risked his life to save countless Jews during the Holocaust. Sidney Carlton, a quite self-centered character in Charles Dickens' *Tale of Two Cities*, took another's place on the gallows. A mean, sleazy, chronically trouble-making soldier walks into certain death by distracting the enemy while his companions flee to safety. These are biblical saints.

The Berlin Wall once separated free West Germany from imprisoned East Germany. Thousands of people died over the years trying to cross that wall to freedom. A small boy is standing on the East side of the wall, his chubby hands wide open. Suddenly, a young communist border guard, known to be a thief and drug dealer, looks all around and then gingerly lifts the child over the fence, into freedom. That young guard was arrested soon after for his compassionate act and shot. He is a biblical saint.

What the Bible is saying is that for all of us, there is, there will be, a golden moment of heroism. It need not be large or dramatic or mighty or earth-shaking. It can be something as quiet as taking the blame for someone else and living with disgrace, or keeping a secret that would destroy another's career—things you might not ordinarily do. But this time, God calls you to do the noble thing, and for some reason, maybe one not even clear to yourself, you say "yes." Or in a lifetime of selfishness, you are presented with the opportunity to do a totally selfless act of love and generosity, and, uncharacteristically, you grasp it. For once in your life, as the saying goes, you do something profoundly decent, and in that moment all your sins are forgotten. No matter what your history, how bad a person you have been, how tepid and indifferent a Christian, you become a biblical saint. Charity covers a multitude of sins.

So, friends, I say to you, there is a moment beckoning you. There is a call calling you. There is a crossroad ahead. Somewhere down the road, there is a selfless act, a chance for heroism, waiting. You may not be a saint according to the standards of our Church today; but if you seize the day and say "yes" to your God-given moment, you will be a saint according to the Bible.

Non-Perishable Food

John 6:24–35

Jesus said, "Do not work for food that perishes but for the food that endures for eternal life."

Think about this; it's a fact of life. What is? The very sobering thought that everything—everything—we now own will be gone one day. Your Wedgwood, your Oriental rugs, your Lexus, your house, your computer, your entertainment console, your cell phone, your CDs, your clothes: everything you and I now own will be gone—passed on, worn out, used up, destroyed, gone. It's a truth we can't dance around. You and I and our material possessions will perish.

In this context, within this truism, a wise and caring voice—that is, the voice of Jesus in the gospel you just heard—gives us a warning not to cling to such "food that perishes," not to put all of our identity there, but rather to work for something that is not perishable, something that endures both here and into eternity. Such as? Such as justice, mercy, truth, forgiveness, fidelity, compassion, love: these are some of the enduring things Jesus has in mind, things that give deep joy on earth and are the passport to heaven. But that is so generic, so general, so broad, isn't it? How can I state Jesus' truth in a way that is more specific, more attractive, more likely to be remembered? The answer, of course, is a story.

But first, I warn you: be careful. The children can enjoy the story as a fairy tale. That's all right. It will work its magic on them without them knowing it. You adults, however, can be seduced into enjoying it as mere entertainment on a muggy day: *that* would be too bad. So I must beseech you to pass beyond the mere entertainment value of this story to grasp its deeper message, for if you pay attention, you will see that it is but a variation of the gospel

There once was a king whose sorrow was unending. Even though he was loved by his queen, worshiped by his subjects and feared by his enemies, he still had no child. "Who will carry on my work, my power, my memory? I must have an heir!" A reward was offered to anyone who could help the royal couple fulfill their dream, while death awaited those who tried and failed. Many tried and many died, but the king and queen remained bitter and childless.

One cold day an old woman came to the king and queen. Shown into the throne room, she proclaimed that a child could be theirs if the king did just one thing. The king became anxious and filled with hope. "And what is that?" he said. The holy woman spoke: "Your Majesty, because there is no system for washing out the human waste, there is much sickness in the land. All waters are the same. Use your army and dig canals through the cities and villages so that the waste may go to one place while the water for drinking and cooking is taken from another source." The king was perturbed: "And this will bring me a child?" The old woman smiled: "It is assured, your majesty."

So the king commanded that a system of canals be built. The pestilence that had attacked the people for generations was now gone, but after many months there still was not a sign of quickening. The old woman was called back before the throne. "You have lied to me. I did as you said, and yet no child is ours. Prepare to die." But the old woman spoke quickly. "My good king, you have only fulfilled part of the requirement. You must now parcel out land to the serfs and peasants, allowing each a lot large enough for both sustenance and sale." "Why should I give what is mine?" the king roared. "So that you might have one with your name to follow," she said softly.

The image of that "one" spoke so deeply to the king that he did as the old woman instructed. Every able-bodied peasant and serf was given his own lot. For the first time in memory, they could feed their families and guests with ease. The king and queen waited, but no child grew between them.

The king's blood boiled beneath his skin as he demanded to have the old woman brought before him, and he condemned her to death. "Your Majesty, you may kill me, but then you will never know if the last requirement will bring fruit." "The last?" Suspicion rolled with hope. "Yes, your Majesty, one last thing will ensure you of an heir. Of this I am sure." "If it does not," said the king with a shaking voice, "your heirs will be denied their mother."

"Have no fear," replied the woman. "The last thing you must do is dismantle your army. For the last two decades, our kingdom has fought war after war. Make lasting treaties with your neighbors and dissolve the force that once protected your aggression." "But my army!" "I give you no choice, Majesty." And so it was done. For the first time in the memory of many, young men remained home behind plow and anvil, and children danced safely by the boarders. Having sacrificed so much, the king was sure that now he would receive his heart's desire. But days turned to months, and months turned to a year with no child. The king had a scaffold erected in the throne room, and the old woman was sent for.

"Now, you will die. Do you have anything to say?" Her eyes looked towards a window and she spoke quietly. "Your Majesty, your wife was barren, as was the land. Your people died of sickness, starvation, and war. Look now at your land. You have given your people health, wealth, and the security of peace. You have given them a better life, and your name is spoken with reverence. It is bestowed upon the children of your subjects and will be passed down to their children and their children's children, and it will be always a name spoken with honor. Through your acts of loving kindness, you will be the father of and remembered by all the children of this land."

The king, whose eyes had followed the old woman's, gazed at the new landscape he had created. Taking her hand, he knew she was right. His children now would number with the stars, and he would be remembered forever.

Without exception, everything we now own will be gone someday. Consider this: since we will be left with nothing material that we now have, what will be our spiritual legacy? The gospel and its twin, the story about the childless king, challenge us: will we be the king who did not get what he wanted but gained everything that he needed to be a saint—and, as a result, not only passed it on but took it with him?

Will we listen to, not questions about our material possessions and portfolios, but questions about our spiritual possessions and portfolios? You know, the familiar questions: did you feed the hungry, give drink to the thirsty, clothe the naked, visit the imprisoned and the sick? These are the questions that resonate on earth and rebound to heaven.

"Do not work for the food that perishes but for the food that endures for eternal life."

Meditations on a Storm

Matthew 14:22–33

This gospel is very rich indeed. It is strangely moving, and it has so many levels that we're not surprised the early Church saved and cherished it. So, let's pick it apart and enter into a kind of communal meditation on it.

"By this time the boat, battered by the waves, was far from the land, for the wind was against them...." There are two images here: one, the boat is Peter's barque, the Church. Once more, it is being tossed about by the waves of scandal, the winds of sin, the churning of failed leadership. The apostles, the bishops, are cringing and terrified. Their leader falters. The Church these days is adrift in troubled waters.

The second image is us. Everyone sitting here in these pews has been battered by the waves—not only the waves of the sex abuse scandal, but by September 11, 2001. Our lives have changed; our security is threatened. But there's more. We have also been tossed about by the shameful, greedy deeds of some corporate CEOs and leaders who let thousands of their employees go down the drain while they walked home with millions in their pockets, who committed lucrative fraud while cheating people of their life's savings.

Tyco's CEO, Dennis Kozlowski, once celebrated, received a $19 million no-interest loan from his company; in doing so, Tyco unknowingly paid for his fancy furnishings, including a $6,000 shower curtain. Sam Waksal, former CEO of ImClone, was indicted on charges of insider trading, bank fraud, and forging a signature. The founder of Adelphia Cable, one of the nation's largest, is taken away in cuffs, along with two of his sons, for looting the company. WorldCom admits to corporate fraud. Enron cooks the books, and Merrill Lynch is accused of helping them. It goes on and on. The greed and hubris and indifference are staggering.

The waves are high and many. Church scandal, terrorist attacks, corporate greed: our spiritual, political, and financial lives have been tossed around like Peter's boat on Lake Genesereth. Some, as we know, have drowned. This gospel lives on.

Jesus said to Peter, "Come." It's a simple, gentle command, one that Jesus gives us daily, the same one he offered to the rich young man elsewhere in the gospel. Think of the ways you obey this command. Think of the ways you avoid this invitation, as did Francis Thompson. You may recall his famous poem, *The Hound of Heaven*, in which he likens Jesus to a bloodhound who pursues him down the roadway of his sins—drink, drugs, illicit sex—until exhausted by life and emptied by excess, he finds himself prone in an alley. In his stupor, Thompson hears those insistent feet follow him there. They stop and stand over him, and in the shadow a voice speaks to him:

"Whom wilt thou find to love ignoble thee,
    Save Me, save only Me?
All which I took from thee I did but take,
    Not for thy harms,
But just that thou might'st seek it in My arms.
    All which thy child's mistake
Fancies as lost, I have stored for thee at home:
    Rise, clasp My hand, and come!"

What makes it difficult for you to clasp that hand? To come to Jesus? What draws you close to him? He has said to Peter and to us, "Come," but we hesitate.

"Peter became frightened." What frightens us the most? What frightens me is waiting for my doctor to call me with the results of my medical tests. What frightens you? Parents are frightened because they can't control the paganism of today's culture, the soft- and hard-core pornography their kids are exposed to everyday, their violent heroes, the overwhelming consumerism, drugs, terrorism, kidnapping. That frightens them.

Seniors are frightened of growing disability, dependency, and death. Mid-lifers are frightened over losing their jobs, seeing their incomes dwindle, their marriages fracture, rejection, betrayal, midlife crisis. Teenagers are frightened of being counted out by the "in" crowd. Children are frightened of the dark, their parents' quarrels and divorces, being picked on, being different, being left out.

What frightens you? For Peter, it was the wind, the waves, and the fear of drowning. We are all frightened one way or another. This gospel lives on. What frightens you?

"Lord, if it is you, command me to come to you on the water." Peter had faith, but, it seems, not enough. Nor do we. "Lord," we cry out, "command me to come to you." We want Jesus, yet we fear him. He might want us altogether too much. After all, we want to be acceptable, American Christians who don't disturb our neighbors or rock the boat. Jesus, on the other hand, wants us to be saints. There is clearly a conflict of interest here.

"Beginning to sink, he cried out." Peter lacked faith, not only faith in Jesus, but, it seems, faith in himself. I think that might be the issue here. "I'm only an ignorant fisherman," he seems to be saying to himself. "I'm from a small village. What does this man want of me? I can't do what he's asking. I'm no saint. I don't have what it takes." Thus he loses confidence and begins to sink—something like us who use false humility to duck God's call to holiness. As we put God off by saying we are not worthy, go bother someone else, do we realize we're sinking?

These are the meditations this gospel evokes. But we must also grasp the underlying hope the gospel gives. That hope is found in the two final lines we should take home with us today, the very point and climax of the story. "Take heart, it is I; do not be afraid." And Jesus stretched out his hand to catch Peter.

Amid the waves stands Jesus. Amid the waves of your lives, dear friends, stands Jesus with an outstretched hand.

That Parable Again!

Matthew 20:1–16

Each year we hear this parable. Each year we find it irritating. Each year we amusedly listen to the preacher trying to square the circle; that is, to make an unfair situation sound fair. Imagine giving someone who works only one hour the same pay as someone who worked twelve hours! It doesn't wash. But if you take the parable out of our modern context and put it in the biblical context—that is, in context with all the other crazy parables that have the same incredible message that slaps us in the face with delightful surprise—it's not as nonsensical as it sounds. Let me review four of the parables that are precise variations on our gospel, and you'll begin to see the point.

First, there is the parable of the unforgiving servant, with its message of God's extraordinary capacity to forgive someone with a huge debt he couldn't possibly pay back. Then there are the familiar stories of the lost sheep, the woman with the lost coin, and the prodigal son. You know them well. In each of these stories, we see how almighty God acts toward us in a way that we would not naturally expect. They all reveal a God who comes to us in love and mercy, not as a harsh judge who justifiably wants to punish us for our sins.

These five parables show God's radical and surprising ways with us. No first-century king, for example, would forgive a huge debt any more than Visa or MasterCard would cancel thousands of dollars of credit card debt. No sensible shepherd would leave ninety-nine sheep at huge risk to go looking for one measly lost animal. No sane woman would sweep her house for hours looking for a single lost coin worth ten cents. And certainly no first-century father would freely forgive his wayward son, running to meet him and then throwing a party to celebrate his return. A proper father would put the son on probation for a while to see if he was serious about repenting.

Likewise in today's parable, the workers who had toiled all day in the oppressive heat felt they had been cheated when they discovered that those who started work only an hour before quitting time received the same pay as they did. But, you see, the same dynamic is at work here as is in the other parables: the late-hour workers are the indebted servant, the lost sheep, the lost coin, the prodigal son. They are all the same character.

In all these stories Jesus is claiming that each of us is of infinite worth to almighty God, no matter who we are or what we have done or not done, how long we have or haven't worked. All fringe, indebted, lost, latecomer folk are given undeserved kindness and mercy. Do you see the point? This is not a parable about fairness or labor-management relations. It's a story about God, a God who leaves ninety-nine to search for one, who sweeps a house for ten cents, who embraces a son who had fled him—and who gives one-hour laborers too much money. It's a story designed to take our breath away and ask, "What kind of a God is this who subverts all human expectations?"

One of my favorite plays is *Les Miserables*, which ran on Broadway for eighteen years. It's a great story, with fabulous music as many of you know. Based on the novel by Victor Hugo, the central character in the story is Jean Valjean, who has been released after nineteen years in prison, a bitter man. He had been sentenced to jail for stealing a loaf of bread to feed the children in his family. Freed at last, Valjean is denied food and lodging in a village, even though he has some money because no one wants an ex-convict around. Finally, a kindly bishop invites him home, offering him a meal and a bed. The bishop insists on putting his finest silver plates on the table used only for special guests when Valjean dines with him.

During the night Valjean wakes up, steals the bishop's silver plates, and sneaks out of the house. The police soon catch him. He lies about the silver plates, saying that the bishop gave them to him as a gift. The police take Valjean back to the bishop's house with the stolen goods. When Valjean returns to the bishop's house in police custody, the bishop exclaims that he is glad to see him because he also wanted to give him the silver candlesticks as well. The gendarmes have no choice but to let him go. This amazing act of forgiveness and mercy makes such a deep impression on Jean Valjean that he is transformed into a new person who spends the rest of his life serving others and showing mercy to them.

Think: the bishop is the forgiving master of the indebted servant, the farmer pursuing the lost sheep, the house sweeper searching for a lousy dime, the father embracing his hippie son. He acts irrationally. Who puts out silverware for a bum? Who pretends that he gave away his silver to the same bum and is glad he's back to claim the candlesticks as well?

Don't you see? The bishop is God; he is the master in today's gospel who acts generously to people who did not earn or deserve his generosity. Now do you catch the point of the parable? God acts in your life and in mine in this same way. God, thank heavens, shows us grace and mercy when we least deserve it, and like Jean Valjean, we are transformed when we truly experience such gracious love. We are freed to serve others, diligently doing good works with no need to keep score any more.

If you want a summary of this gospel, here it is: there were cries from the lost servant, the lost sheep, the lost coin, the lost son, and the lost workers. This parable says that, unbelievably, their cries were heard by God, who lost both his mind and his heart, went out, and found them.

From No to Maybe to Yes

Matthew 21:28–32

Ask someone about Catholicism and the responses range, as in today's gospel parable, from no to maybe to yes. Let's explore all three this morning.

As for the "no," there are those who out and out hate the Catholic Church and shout "No!" at every opportunity. Anti-Catholic prejudice is a large cottage industry, especially among the media and university intellectuals. Pierce University in Los Angeles, for instance, had recently scheduled two lectures by a woman who was totally without credentials—except for her hatred of the Church. Her topic was "Crime and Immorality in the Catholic Church." Someone pointed out that there was no comparable lecture offered on "Crime and Immorality in the Protestant Church" or "…in the Synagogue."

There's more. A billboard in Oregon hosts this blazing logo: "The Pope is the Anti-Christ". HBO's *Sex in the City* aired a segment called "Unoriginal Sin" that featured an unmarried mother who is going to have her baby baptized because the father's mother—pictured as a stereotypical Irish drunk—is afraid that, otherwise, the child will go to hell. The baby's mother agrees to the baptism as long as there is no mention of Christianity. This is standard anti-Catholicism, the standard "nos" that are daily fare in medialand.

On the everyday level, there are people whose anti-Catholic sentiments are so deeply ingrained from childhood, from their own church's teaching, they find it difficult to believe that many accusations against the Catholic Church are distorted or simply not true. Says one man:

My whole focus centered on my hatred of the Catholic Church. I insisted that Catholics had added seven books to the Bible. I warned people about the different ways Catholics interpret Scripture and the way they try to earn their salvation through prayers and good works. I mocked them for worshiping Mary and praying to statues of saints as if they were gods. I laughed at their formal prayers and Rosary beads. I was horrified at the way Catholics tried to re-crucify Jesus Christ during every Mass. I believed that putting the body of Christ on a cross was an insult to the Resurrection. I thought the idea of confessing your sins to a priest was all insult to God.

So much for the "nos."

Then, in between "nos" and "yeses," there are the people who struggle with "maybe." One of these people puts it this way:

Right now I am just struggling with my faith in general. Sometimes I feel such a distance between myself and God. I don't seem to be able to close it. I just don't understand why some people seem so secure in their relationship with God and why it is such a struggle for me. I don't want it to be this way but it just is.

Here is another opinion:

My mother is a Protestant, and my father is a lapsed Catholic. I was raised in no religion at all. The first time I stepped into a church was when a Baptist friend dragged me. To say the least, I was confused. I drifted into Wicca, but probably I was more agnostic than anything. I married an atheist who ridiculed every religion. Within three months my whole life fell apart. I got into a nasty car wreck. I was diagnosed with rheumatoid arthritis. I lost my job and got divorced. I knew there had to be a reason why my life had gone this way. I started researching lots of religions but nothing seemed to fit. Most religions either seemed to say it was my fault that bad things happened, or it was my fault for not believing in their God. One day I ended up on a Catholic website. I started reading Catholic books. These books were filled with people who seemed to have gone through some of the same things I did, and they still had faith. Even when bad things happened, they still praised God. I was astounded. They knew life was hard, but they had the help of Someone who was always right there with them. I wanted that Someone in my life.

Among the maybes are also lapsed Catholics who every once in a while look over their shoulders:

My husband and I were married in a Catholic Church because my parents were paying for the wedding. After a few years of not going to church at all, we started talking about children and decided that we should really belong to some church. Neither of us really cared that much about religion. We began to shop for a church, and we settled on a Methodist church because we liked the choir. It was also the predominant church in our area and so it really helped us in business. It was hard on my family. My mother still sends me holy cards. Sometimes I think that I would like to go back to the Catholic Church, but I know that my husband would be opposed to it.

Finally, there are those who say "yes," like this woman:

I became a Catholic when my son was making his First Communion, but it wasn't until four or five years ago when I was sick, that I really felt as if I needed God. That's when I said, "Okay, here I am. Help me through this." And he did. That's when I realized converting to Catholicism was the right thing. That's when I found myself stopping at church for Mass at lunchtime—not just on Sunday—and I really wanted to be there. I really felt a connection more than ever.

Did you know that over 150,000 people each year in this

country alone become Catholics? And often, these folks are from the elite ranks. In the last century there were very famous names such as Robert Hugh Benson, Ronald Knox, J. R. R. Tolkien, Maria Von Trapp, Gerard Manley Hopkins, Christopher Dawson, G. K. Chesterton, Eric Gill, Graham Greene, Evelyn Waugh, Francios Mauriac, Jacques Maritan, and Sigrid Undset.

Closer to home, famous converts include Dorothy Day, advocate for the poor who is being considered for canonization; Thomas Merton, the trappist whose spiritual writings have influenced so many; Avery Dulles, son of Secretary of State John Foster Dulles, who became not only a Catholic, but a Jesuit and now a cardinal; Sidney Callahan, a noted journalist; Jim Forrest, peace activist and author; John Michael Talbot, a Christian singer and composer; Cherry Boone, daughter of Pat Boone; Malcolm Muggeridge, editor of *Punch*; Annie Dillard, the Pulitzer Prize winner; Barnard Nathanson, once a Jewish doctor; and Scott Hahn, a former minister.

The bottom line is that there are those who, like the son in today's gospel, say "yes" and never get around to doing something. These are the Catholics who have drifted away from the Church or have failed to keep up with their faith. There are those who, like the other son in the gospel, say "no" but then finally get around to embracing the faith. These are the converts and those born Catholic who delve deeper into their faith. In between the "yeses" and the "nos" are the "maybes": the perplexed, the searchers, the nostalgic Catholics who have left.

There is one important thought I must leave you with. In all these groups—those who say "no," who say "yes," and who say "maybe"—their response is almost always influenced by another Catholic. People who encounter scandalous, ignorant, or indifferent Catholics are repelled. People who encounter joyful Catholics who believe and can give an account of their faith are attracted and converted. I guess, therefore, the bottom line is this: can you give an account of your faith? Have you kept up with your understanding of the Church and its teachings? When was the last time you read a book or a magazine about your faith?

Advent and Lent are just around the corner. I suggest that these are good times for all of us to do some basic reading about the faith. It is really up to each one of us to learn more about our faith so that we can do our duty as Catholics which, when you come right down to it, is to confirm the "yeses," confront the "nos," and encourage the "maybes."

The Lord Is My Shepherd

Psalm 23

Even though I walk in the dark valley, I fear no evil; for you are at my side with your rod and your staff that give me courage.

This verse of the responsorial psalm, from one of our favorite psalms, sets the tone for this morning's reflection on God's word. This man helps us as he writes:

Once, while visiting in Arizona, I went jogging down a dirt road that wound through the sagebrush, and [I] stumbled upon an eating disorder clinic that caters to the wealthy. I veered off my dusty desert trail onto a groomed cinder track, which, I soon discovered, was a twelve-step trail. Signs with motivational slogans such as "expect a miracle" lined the trail. And as I continued to jog along, I found myself proceeding through each step in AA-based recovery plan. Placards on the trail urged me to confess that my body is out of control and that I am powerless to control my eating habits. The trail ended at a cemetery of tiny carved grave markers. I stopped to read each grave. "Here lies my fear of intimacy" someone named Donna had written on September 15.... She decorated the tombstone in yellow, red, and blue paint. Others buried such things as cigarettes, an obsession with chocolate, diet pills, a lack of self-discipline, the need to control others, a habit of lying.

The man who found this graveyard then asked himself: if he attended a spiritual disorder clinic and took this walk each day, how many tombstones would he leave along the trail? "What do *I* need to bury?" he thought. It's a good question. I suspect that if each of us here asked this question, the answers would be as varied as the number of people. "What do I need to bury?"

Were I to try to find one spiritual corpse common to us all, I suspect I would not be far off the mark if I named the need to bury our conviction that our sins and shortcomings disconnect us from God; that our moral failures put us beyond his reach and his concern; that God's relationship with us switches on or off depending on our behavior; that somehow our daily betrayals can deter God from loving us.

This quite unbiblical attitude is indeed common. To see if there were exceptions, I tested the theory on two friends of mine who work in inner city ministry in Philadelphia. This is what I said to each of them: "Typically, I find that most Catholic people I know say that when we sin, or backslide, we so disrupt our relationship with God that God withdraws, as it were; and they themselves run the other way away from God, feeling unworthy. Now, you work with people who live with failure every day. Have you found that backsliding draws them further from God or presses them toward God?"

Bud, who works among drug addicts, had an immediate answer:

Without question, it pushes them toward God. I could tell you story after story of addicts who give in to their addiction, knowing what a terrible thing they are doing to themselves and their families. Watching them, I understand the power of evil in this world, evil that they want above all else to resist but cannot. Yet those moments of weakness are the very moments when they are most likely to turn to God, to cry out in desperation. They have failed terribly. Now what? Can they get up and walk again, or do they stay paralyzed? Through the grace of Lord, some of them do get up.

Then he added something that has always stuck with me. He said:

In fact, I've decided there is one key in determining whether individual drug addicts can be cured: if they deeply believe they are a forgivable child of God. Not a failure-free child of God but a forgivable one.

My other friend, David, who directs a hospice for AIDS patients, agreed:

I have met no more spiritual people than the men in this house who face death and know that in some ways they brought the disease on themselves. Most got the HIV virus through drug use and sexual promiscuity. Their lives are defined by failure. I cannot explain it, but these men have a spirituality, a connection with God, that I've seen nowhere else.

I went away thinking of Francis de Sales, who wrote, "Now the greater our knowledge of our own misery, the more profound will be or confidence in the goodness and mercy of God, for mercy and misery are so closely related that the one cannot be exercised without the other." Therese of Lisieux added that, "prayer arises, if at all, from incompetence, our sense of incompleteness that drives us to God. Grace comes as a gift, received only by those with open hands, and often failure is what causes us to open our hands."

You see what I'm trying to get across? Our failures, moral and social, do not separate us from the love of God. Our descent into dark deeds, our fondness for sin, does not force God to give up on us.

Perhaps this will help. A minister tells this story.

I once knew a little boy. When he was seven years old, this boy made a mistake that left a deep impression on him. He walked into a drug store and tried to steal some penny candy. He was unsuccessful but instead of being reported to the police, was made to go home and tell his parents what he had done. This task was the most difficult he had ever faced. He had fleeting thoughts of breaking his arm on purpose, of running in front of a car, of doing anything that would relieve him of the dreaded conversation with his parents. The boy's father had one immediate reaction, "My son is a criminal." Those words cut to the heart. They were terrible, but they were true: seven years old—a criminal. But the boy's weeping mother took only a few seconds to respond to that verdict. "My son is not a criminal; he's going to be a preacher."

I was that boy, and my mother's response was a lesson in love. My father loved me too, loved me enough to say what was true. I had done something that, at the moment, defined me as a thief. But he did not say the whole truth; my mother saw the possibility in me, saw what I could do and not just what I had done."

My dear fellow sinners, my dear fellow failures, there is much to be buried in the graveyard of our spiritual disorder clinic. You and I know what moral failures need to be entombed forever. But of all the grave markers that ought to be there, surely there must be one for believing that our sins and failures forever define us; that God no longer loves us or sees possibilities in us; that misery casts out mercy rather than invites it in.

Not so: even though we walk in the dark valley of sin, along the chasm of failure, through the bottomless hole of addiction, God is there. With rod and staff, he endlessly offers possibilities, hope, a better future.

The Lord is indeed my Shepherd. I shall not want his presence. He is ever at my side, even at my worst moments. He forever sees not what I have done, but what I can do.

The Big Picture

Matthew 22:15–21

Evil these days, it seems, is pervasive, upfront, center stage. It is
as blaring as corporate corruption at Tyco,
as devastating as layoffs at Lucent,
as dark as the drunken children in Scarsdale,
as hurtful as spousal betrayal in New Jersey,
as shameless as abuse in Boston,
as suffocating as homelessness in Chicago,
as tyrannizing as addiction in California,
as scarring as divorce in Las Vegas,
as jarring as war-talk in Washington,
as explosive as collapsing towers in New York,
as loud as a car bomb in Indonesia, and
as sharp as a sniper's bullet in Maryland.

Evil, like some cosmic, malicious spider, webs our lives.
We're all caught in it. A priest from New York speaks for us all
when he stated that when he saw the burning towers at what is
now called Ground Zero, he knew instinctively that he was wit-
nessing what Pope John Paul II referred to as *mysterium iniqui-
tatis*, the mystery of evil.

The mystery of evil: deep, nonstop, pervasive, enormous,
mind-boggling evil. It seems that almost every day we are faced
with its terrible reality. From where we stand, it is as if Satan had

been let loose on the world. We feel scared, unsafe, on edge in an unpredictable world. We no longer feel secure from terrorists, family betrayals, or sudden, unexpected violence as we collectively keep looking over our shoulders. As we glance around, we are silently asking the question everyone has asked since Noah's flood: "Where is God in all this evil?" Yes, even we who come to church hoping that somehow, some way, we can catch a hint of an answer, that there *is* an answer and, if there isn't, we want to know, "where do we go from here?" We are nervous, frightened.

There is, alas, no direct answer to questions of God's presence when evil so brazenly stalks us. But there are perspectives, a way of looking at things. For example, looking at the Bible, from the first chapter of Genesis to the last chapter of Revelation, we detect two main power streams in the history of this planet. The first stream is evil, which seizes what is good and despoils it. Since the Fall, we live in a world dominated by powers that are tilted toward evil.

In opposition, however, God unleashes a second stream of power to redeem what evil has spoiled. But here's the catch: at least for the time being, God has chosen to exercise his power through the most unlikely of foot soldiers, that is, flawed human beings. Because of this tactic, it may sometimes appear as if God is losing the battle. But, remember, God is in it for the long haul; and the promise is that the quiet virtue of flawed people and the power of God's grace will someday vanquish evil, that silently but effectively the simple decency and everyday heroism of people will redeem good from what is bad.

There will be victory. The hard thing is, we can't see this now because of our limited perspective, like seeing nothing but dense trees at the bottom of the mountain. But at the very top— catching sight of the clouds, the whole forest, the lakes, the meadows, the waterfalls—we get a different perspective. So it is that, for the moment, we are seeing only partly. *That's* what gives us doubts and increases our anxiety.

But now and then we do catch the hints of the larger picture. Fr. Jim Martin, a Jesuit who was at Ground Zero, points, for example, to the stories of self-sacrifice from the heroic passengers on Flight 93 to the firefighters who selflessly rushed into doomed buildings. Remember the now-famous photograph that showed a young firefighter, burdened with his heavy gear, laboring up a staircase as others made their way down? Against every human instinct of self-preservation, he went into danger to save others. No thought of fame or celebrity status; no thought of self. Just a willingness to perform heroic deeds without the promise of reward or the certainty of survival.

This is not to say that this man or the rescue workers who lost their lives at the World Trade Center were all saints. But that is precisely the point: they were everyday human beings who showed us the way God is present in an evil world. And they are legion. It has always been this way. The truth is that in this world of spectacular evil, God's presence is silently here. Only it's unspectacular,

as quiet as a baby's breathing in a manger as killing soldiers rush by,

as soft as a healing of a woman about to be stoned,

as simple as a whisper of forgiveness to tax cheat,

as slow as a labored promise of paradise on a blood-drenched, insect infested hill called Golgotha,

as silent as life issuing from a tomb,

as subtle as calling the name of a woman who comes to mourn the dead, and

as dreamlike as the Spirit falling on the minds and into the hearts of fearful, discouraged disciples.

Outside of and beyond the limelight of evil, God's daily presence is

as steady as a guard at the crossing,

as faithful as a nurse by a bedside,

as tender as a caregiver to the elderly,

as firm as the hug of a child,

as expected as the morning's first prayer, and

as predictable as those who daily give us clean sheets, food on the table, clothes on our backs, and comfort in times of stress and tragedy.

Occasionally at times, that presence is as broad and as eye-catching as firefighters and Mother Teresas.

When you get a sense of being overwhelmed by so much evil, when you are nervous over silent danger, when you are concerned about another war and the killing and the violence and the circuses that sell our newspapers and fill our screens, remember that, like so many Snow-White dwarfs—or if you want to be more updated, like so many Hobbits—there are countless and nameless people tunneling, as it were, under the landslide of evil. One day they will subvert the landslide; one day they will break through. In the long run, in the big picture, there is light at the end of the tunnel as sure as there was a resurrection after Calvary's darkness.

So be faithful to virtue. Be faithful to your corner of the world, whether at home, at work, or at school, and realize that your being there means God is present. Your honesty and your truth and your witness hasten the breakthrough and increase hope for a weary people—just as your dishonesty and falsehood add to the pile of evil and increase despair.

You count. I guess that's the bottom line when it comes to the mystery of evil. You count. In times of public evil, that's the ultimate answer to the question, "Where is God?" Softly, quietly, faithfully, unobtrusively, your life, your deeds give the answer: "Here I am!"

Parable of the Ten Virgins

Matthew 25:1-13

There is no doubt about it: the first Christians fully expected Jesus to return soon, very soon. It was much on their minds. You really couldn't blame them. After all, Jesus had said quite clearly: "As the lightening comes from the east and flashes in the west, so will be the coming of the Son of Man....Truly, this generation will not pass away until all these things take place."

So St. Paul, following Jesus' lead, unhesitatingly expected Christ's return in his lifetime and wrote about it, as did Mark and Matthew and the rest of the first Christian authors. But they were eventually doomed to disappointment as days, weeks, months, and years went by, and Jesus was a no-show. Some began to wonder if Jesus were coming back at all; if so, when? And, if when, then how were they to conduct themselves?

Matthew's gospel about the ten virgins is his answer to this dilemma. It is aimed precisely at those who were losing heart, losing faith, and giving up. He offers a parable from Jesus that basically warns his followers to be always ready, no matter what the schedule. The Lord, like the bridegroom, will indeed come, but he will come when we least expect him. So don't be foolish. Be prepared.

Christians have been prepared for 2000 years now. Even with a no-show and a weaker sense of urgency than the early

135

Christians, we still recite every Sunday a Creed that proclaims, "He will come again to judge the living and the dead"—although dulled by familiarity and the lack of signs, we don't pay much attention to what we're saying.

Nevertheless, this hasn't prevented a consistent and steady stream of folk who, in every century since the first, seem to know what no one else knows: exactly when Jesus is coming back. History is rampant with endless predictions that have never come true.

Yet, in spite of the consistently obvious lack of fulfillment and consistently failed timetables, people still listen to the sincere but misguided prophesiers. Even today. For example, as many of you are aware, the latest warnings and timetable are to be found in the phenomenally best-selling *Left Behind* series by Tim LeHaye and Joseph Jenkins. These books sell in the millions and are always on the *New York Times* bestseller lists. The content of these books is as far from Catholic and mainline Protestant teaching as you can get. They are about as accurate as Hal Lindsey's bestselling book, *The Late Great Planet Earth*—which is to say, they are full of eccentric, false, and misleading readings of Scripture, not to mention a good peppering of anti-Catholicism.

But far out as they are, their very popularity, even among Catholics, shows that interest in Jesus' second coming is very much alive—and maybe, subconsciously, even desired. Why not? Look around you: there is so much terrorism, so much war, so much divorce, so much pornography, so much drug abuse, so much abortion, so much child abuse, so much poverty, so much addiction, so much genocide, so much unfairness, so much corruption, so much trouncing of Christian values, that we simply yearn for Christ to come and put an end to it all. Who can blame people for secretly wanting Christ to come and punish the evildoers, lift, as he promised, the battered downtrodden to high places, and restore fundamental human decency and dignity?

Understandable as this yearning might be, the truth of the

matter seems to be that, like the community Matthew address-es in today's gospel, we're stuck with the "meanwhile." Until that desired Second Coming occurs, what do we do? How do Christians live? Matthew's answer gives us a way to handle the meanwhile. In the parable of the wise and foolish virgins, he offers us two themes: be prepared and be recognized.

First, be prepared not only for the visitation of Jesus in judg-ment and death, but also for his visitations in life. Jesus does come very often, in many ways while we are alive: the inspira-tion to help those in need; the out-of-the-blue sense that we should pray; the subterranean, restless gnawing that asks, as we rush through life, is this all that there is?; the unease in the back of the mind that says I should get out of what is stifling me, leave the situation that is stealing my heart; the barely con-scious question, as I deposit my check, whether this money was made at the price of another piece of my soul; the sudden impulse to do good, to be noble, less selfish.

Then there are the more insistent attention-getters: the death of a friend, the onslaught of an illness, seeing an old person in the mirror, the flash of beauty, the awesomeness of a canyon, the falling-asleep-in-your-arms of your first child or grandchild. All these common occurrences are inspirations of the Holy Spirit. These, my friends, are visits from Jesus. If we would only know, stay awake, recognize, and embrace these times when the groom arrives, we would be prepared indeed, no matter when the final visit. This is Matthew's first lesson.

The second lesson in Matthew's gospel is to live in such a way as to be recognized as Jesus' spiritual kin. The truly terrible words Jesus says in the parable are, "Amen, I say to you, I do not know you." I don't think there could be any more terrifying words in the entire gospel. Jesus not know me? I, a baptized Catholic, a member of his Church? Why doesn't he know me?

The clue comes in another part of the gospel, when his moth-er and his brethren want to see Jesus but can't get near because of the crowd. So they send word up the line, and finally some-one near him says to Jesus, "Excuse me, but your mother and your brethren are here to see you." But Jesus turns around, gestures to the crowd, and says for everyone to hear, "Who are my mother and my brother and my sister? Those who do the will of my Father are my real mother and brother and sister."

Our personal faith and good works, not card-carrying membership, configure us to Christ and make us mother, brother, and sister. That is to say, they make us instantly recognizable. You get this truth of personal responsibility quite pointedly in what likely startles you. It's the place in the parable where the foolish virgins ask the five wise ones to share some of their oil. Remember? And, much to our consternation, the five wise ones reply, "No way!" That sounds terribly selfish from a group of supposedly wise virgins. But they're wiser than you think: the fact is that the oil stands for faith and good works, and these are simply not transferable. You can't borrow the oil of faith. You can't borrow another's good works. You must respond to God's call yourself.

So it comes down to this. For us who live in the "meanwhile," Matthew has left a Jesus-story. In summary: once upon a time, there were ten virgins. Five were wise and stayed alert to receive the Groom in his many visitations. As a result, they kept their oil supply full by faith and good works. When the Groom came the final time, it was a family reunion; the household door was open.

Five of the virgins were foolish and always terribly distracted. "There's never enough time," they exclaimed as they went off in many directions, leaving their loved ones neglected, the poor uncared for, and their neighbors unaffirmed in the ways of God. They simply never slowed down enough to listen to the whisperings of the Spirit or to fill their lamps with faith and good works. They had, alas, become strangers.

"I do not recognize you" were the last words they heard before the door was shut.

Learning to Enjoy Holland

Matthew 25:14–30

Listen carefully to my version of today's gospel for I want to turn it on its head so we can all take something home with us. Once upon a time, a rich man gave three people some money. To the first he gave five thousand dollars. This woman went and invested it and, with the profit she made, took a long-desired trip to Italy and had a marvelous time. To the second he gave two thousand dollars, and this man invested the money as well. He too then went off to sunny Italy to enjoy the wonderful sights and food.

To the third the rich man gave one thousand dollars. He looked at it, knew it was far less than what the others had received, felt bad that he didn't get as much as they did, and knew it wouldn't be enough to get him to Italy for any length of time. But a friend suggested that it would at least get him to Holland. It wasn't Italy, said the friend, but it was a nice country, and he would enjoy it. But the third man felt too disappointed and hurt, so he hid the money in a cookie jar and let it stay there. He then went about his life with sadness as his constant companion, mourning his misfortune, wondering why the rich man seemed to love the others more than him.

Too bad about the man with the one thousand dollars. I feel sorry for him, as we all must. Nevertheless, his friend was right:

even though it isn't Italy, Holland really is a lovely country, and he should have gone there, for he would have found treasures and joys he didn't expect.

You are wondering what I'm getting at, and I will tell you. But first, hold my story in mind while you listen carefully to another. When my sister gave birth to her third child, my nephew, who has Down Syndrome, she received this letter from the Mental Retardation Association. It reads:

When you are going to have a baby, it's like your planning a vacation to Italy. You are all excited about seeing the Coliseum, the Michelangelos, the gondolas of Venice. You get a whole bunch of guidebooks. You learn a few phrases in Italian so you can order in restaurants and get around. When it comes time, you excitedly pack your bags, head for the airport, and take off for Italy...only when you land the stewardess announces, "Welcome to Holland." You look at one another in disbelief and shock saying, "Holland? What are you talking about—Holland? I signed up for Italy!" But they explain that there has been a change of plans, and the plane has landed in Holland—and there you must stay. "But I don't know anything about Holland, and I don't want to learn!"

But you do stay. You go out and buy some new guidebooks. You learn some new phrases in a whole new language, and you meet people you never knew existed. But the important thing is that you are not in a filthy, plague-infested slum full of pestilence and famine. You are simply in another place, a different place than you had planned. It's slower paced than Italy; but after you have been there awhile and have half a chance to catch your breath, you begin to discover that Holland has windmills....Holland has tulips....Holland even has Rembrandts.

But everyone else you know is busy coming and going from Italy. And they're bragging about what a great time they had there. And for the rest of your life you will say, "Yes, that was where I was going, that's where I was suppose to go, that is what I had planned." And the pain of that will never go away. And you have to accept that pain because the loss of that dream, the loss of that plan, is a very significant loss. But if you spend your life mourning the fact that you didn't go to Italy, you will never be free to enjoy the very special, the very lovely things about Holland.

Now, do you get my point and understand why I told you both stories? This gospel is really about love, about how God so deeply loves us that, even when things don't turn out the way we wanted, there are hidden treasures of grace and avenues of growth we never suspected. The gospel says to all of us who only received one thousand dollars—to all of us whose life did not quite turn out as we hoped, whose plans went awry, whose lost dreams never will be retrieved, whose children are less than perfect—that we still have talents, we still have gifts, we are still wrapped tightly in the Father's love.

In fact, in our very disappointment, in our own Holland we can find Rembrandts—which, as you know, they don't have in Italy. That is to say, we can often find spiritual depth and a richer love that we could never have found if everything turned out as we wished. For so many of us, the message of today's gospel is not to wallow in our sad misfortune and fractured dreams, not to bury our hopes, not to keep looking over our shoulder longing for Italy. We're in Holland now offers the gospel. Invest. Enjoy. For there is a unique and wonderful God-love there not to be found anywhere else.

And that is the truth. Amen.

Endtime Surprises

Matthew 25:31–46

The coach had put together the perfect team for the Detroit Lions. The only thing that was missing was a good quarterback. He had scouted all the colleges and even the high schools, but he couldn't find a ringer quarterback who could ensure a Super Bowl win.

Then one night, while watching CNN, he saw a war-zone scene in Bosnia. In one corner of the background, he spotted a young Bosnian soldier with a truly incredible arm. He threw a hand grenade straight into an eleventh-story window 200 yards away: ka-boom! He threw another hand grenade into a group of ten soldiers 100 yards away: ka-blooey! Then a car passed, going ninety miles an hour: bulls-eye! "I've got to get this guy!" the coach said to himself. "He has the perfect arm!"

So he brings the man to the States and teaches him the great game of football, and the Lions go on to win the Super Bowl. The young Bosnian is hailed as the great hero of football. When the coach asks him what he wants now, all the young man wants to do is call his mother.

"Mom," he says into the phone, "I just won the Super Bowl!"

"I don't want to talk to you," the old woman says. "You deserted us. You are not my son."

"But, Mother," the young man pleads, "I just won the greatest sporting event in the world. I'm here among thousands of my adoring fans."

"No, let me tell you," his mother retorts. "At this very

moment, there are gunshots all around us. The neighborhood is a pile of rubble. Your two brothers were beaten within an inch of their lives last week, and this week your sister was assaulted in broad daylight."

The old lady pauses, and then tearfully says, "I'll never forgive you for making us move to Detroit!"

This gives you an idea of how the original listeners heard today's gospel—not the laughter part, but the twist, the unexpected, the surprise part. "Lord"—said with raised eyebrows—"when did we see you hungry or thirsty or naked or in prison and not minister to your needs?" And the punch line: "What you did not do for one of these least ones, you did not do for me."

This gospel, then, provokes two thoughts. One is that we must pay attention to what we call the sins of omission. In spite of our confession at the beginning of this and every Mass—"for what I have done and what I have failed to do"—we are often so busy avoiding evil that we fail to do good. That's why in confession many people will say to the priest, "I can't think of anything I've done wrong. I'm sure I have sinned, but I haven't killed anybody or stolen. I'm sure I've done a bunch of little things but I can't think of any." They're passing over the sins of omission.

As someone once paraphrased the essence of today's passage: "I was hungry and you said apply for food stamps. I was homeless and you said there is a shelter in town. I was lonely and you said get a Sony Walkman. I was beaten and you said avoid dark alleys. I was naked and you said a local church has clothes. I was sick and you said apply for Medicaid. I was illiterate and you said there are library cards. I was poor and you said God loves the poor. I was imprisoned and you said try the parole board. I was depressed and you gave me a smiley button. I was dying and you said there is eternal life."

Closer to home, there are the daily challenges of reaching out to others, tithing, going the extra mile, volunteering for worthy causes, praying for one's personal and national enemies, dropping by to see if someone needs something, deciding to cut down on Christmas spending and give the unspent money to, say, Catholic Relief Services which will, in our name, feed the hungry, give drink to the thirsty, clothe the freezing, and provide medicine for the sick. By acknowledging our sins of omission, we are challenged to break out of our own self-satisfied and self-contained world. Jesus' disturbing parable reminds us that it's not what we do that will do us in, but what we don't do.

The second thought is quite sober, almost novel, although we often give it lip service. We will be judged. Think about that. We will be judged. Someone outside of us will judge us. The very notion grates on our modern sensitivities. In our value-neutral society where we like to believe that there is no higher standard of judgment than our own self-measurements, this gospel has the effrontery to remind us that we shall be judged by Another with a capital "A."

In the National Shrine in Washington, which many of you have visited, there is a powerful, striking, and huge mosaic of Jesus over the main high altar. He is holding a lightening bolt in one hand, and he looks stern, something like Zeus on Mount Olympus. Some people are put off by it. They find it too frightening, or at least not what they were taught to expect. That's because they were raised only on a scaled-down, New Age sweet Jesus, you know, the benign shepherd with the wavy hair walking through the meadows with a little lamb and speaking beautiful words to beautiful people.

But there's more to Jesus than that for, as we shall soon declare in our Creed, "he will come to judge the living and the dead." And there will be no more sweet talk but rather soul-searing words: "Depart from me, you accursed, into the eternal fire!" Why such harsh words? The Judge himself supplies the answer. "Because what you did not do for one of these least ones, you did not do for me." In our world of nonjudgmental, "my conscience is my guide" morality, this parable powerfully makes its point: we shall be judged on what we have done and on what we have failed to do.

Today is an ending. This feast of Christ the King, as you know, now completes the Church's year. For fifty-one Sundays we have heard the good news of Christ among us declaring over and over again in many ways and by many deeds, his unconditional love for us. We have heard how far he will go to both embrace and chase us, even when we flee him.

Today, the fifty-second and final Sunday of the Church year reverses the equation, asking how we have embraced and chased Jesus in the poor and the spiritually needy. This judgment-time question prepares us for the second chance of Advent, which begins next week.

Choosing Compromise or Christ

John 18:33–37

The gospel today is a rich tapestry of a scene, fraught with drama and color as the two protagonists square off. Pilate is nervous. Seven times he's in and out of the praetorium, the governor's residence, commuting between the people and the prisoner. In his heart he knows Jesus is innocent—after all, his wife had a dream about that—but in his head he knows he must play the game of politics. So he mixes up a compromise from the two: he washes his hands to satisfy his conscience, then sends Jesus off to his death to satisfy his constituents.

Thus does Pontius Pilate come down in history as the great compromiser, the symbol of all those who bend their principles and buy a little acceptance time, and so continue to sentence the Christ to his death day after day.

On the other hand, there are those who would not—do not—compromise, those who demonstrate in their lives and sometimes by their deaths, that, given a choice, Christ is King and they will follow him. When Jesus really matters to such people, where Christ is truly King, the compromises fall away before the truth. Let me share with you some of their stories.

In April, 1940, Nazi Germany invaded Denmark. There was little resistance because the Danes felt it would be hopeless to try, and a puppet Danish government got on as best it could.

But then, in 1943, German policy toughened. It was decided to impose on Denmark the same final solution that was being exercised in the other occupied territories, that is, to exterminate all Jews. Suddenly, there was a remarkable transformation in the people. German officers leaked the plan to the Danish resistance. Escape routes were quickly organized. Jewish people tell how complete strangers approached them in the streets with the keys to their houses so they could hide. Train guards and boat captains joined the plan.

Within a few weeks all but a few of the 7,000 Jews in Denmark had been whisked over the Oresund to safety in Sweden. Some even tell how their escape boats were boarded and searched by German patrol vessels, yet the Germans let them through. For many Danes it eventually meant the concentration camp and death. But faced with the very human need of the Jews, it seemed that a whole nation, and many Germans too, turned its back on political compromise and performed a true and great act of love.

There's another hero of World War II, a loyal, young German soldier named Joseph Schultz, who was sent to Yugoslavia shortly after that country was invaded. One day, while Schultz was out on patrol, the sergeant called out eight names, his among them. The eight thought they were going on a routine patrol. As they hitched up their rifles, they came over a hill, still not knowing what their mission was. There stood eight Yugoslavians on the brow of the hill, five men and three women. It was only when the soldiers got about fifty feet away from them, when any marksman could shoot out the eye of a pheasant, that the soldiers realized what their mission was.

The eight soldiers were lined up. The sergeant barked out, "Ready!" and they lifted up their rifles; "Aim," and they got their sights. Suddenly, in the silence that prevailed, there was the thud of a rifle butt against the ground. The sergeant, the seven other soldiers, and those eight Yugoslavians stopped and looked as Private Joseph Schultz walked toward the Yugoslavians. His sergeant called after him and ordered him to come back, but he pretended not to hear. Instead, he walked the fifty feet to the mound of the hill, and he joined hands with the eight Yugoslavians.

There was a moment of silence; then the sergeant yelled, "Fire!" And Private Joseph Schultz died, mingling his blood with those innocent men and women. Do you know what was found later on his body, sewn into his coat? An excerpt from St. Paul: "Love does not delight in evil, but rejoices in the truth. It always protects, always trusts, always hopes, and always perseveres." Christ was king for Private Schultz, not Hitler.

Here's another instance. During the prime days of the struggle for racial integration in the South, black civil rights workers—the freedom riders, as they were called—would travel on buses from city to city as they challenged the segregation laws. Sometimes they were greeted with violence; often they were arrested.

In one town, a bus was halted by the police, and the passengers were booked and jailed. While they were there, the jailers did everything possible to make them miserable and to break their spirits. They tried to deprive them of sleep with noise and light during the nights. They intentionally oversalted their food to make it distasteful. They gradually took away their mattresses, one by one, hoping to create conflict over the remaining ones. Eventually the strategies seemed to be taking hold. Morale in the jail cells was beginning to sag.

One day, looking around at his dispirited fellow prisoners, one of the jailed leaders softly began to sing a spiritual. Slowly, others joined in until the whole group was singing at the top of their voices. The puzzled jailers felt the entire cellblock vibrating with the sounds of a joyful gospel song. When they went to see what was happening, the prisoners triumphantly pushed the remaining mattresses through the cell bars, saying, "You can take our mattresses, but you can't take our souls."

It was the hymn singers who were in jail, but it was the jailers who were guilty. It was the prisoners who were suffering, but the jailers who were defeated. It was the prisoners who were in a position of weakness, but it was the broken and bigoted world of the jailers, and of all the Pontius Pilates of history, who were perishing.

We have to ask ourselves, what makes some people take such stands in life while others do not? What makes them spurn the role of Pilate while others embrace it? I think a large part of the answer is found in what people observe and learn in the home, what they witnessed while growing up. Like:

When you thought I wasn't looking, I saw you hang my first painting on the refrigerator, and I wanted to paint another one.

When you thought I wasn't looking, I saw you feed a stray cat, and I thought it was good to be kind to animals.

When you thought I wasn't looking, I saw you make my favorite cake just for me, and I knew that little things are special things.

When you thought I wasn't looking, I heard you say a prayer, and I believed there is a God I could always talk to.

When you thought I wasn't looking, I felt you kiss me good night, and I felt loved.

When you thought I wasn't looking, I saw tears come from your eyes, and I learned that sometimes things hurt, but it's all right to cry.

When you thought I wasn't looking, I saw that you cared, and I wanted to be everything that I could be.

When you thought I wasn't looking, I looked, and wanted to say thanks for all the things I saw when you thought I wasn't looking.

In her book *Out of Africa*, Isak Dinesen tells the story of a young man from the Kikuyu tribe who worked on her farm for three months. One day, he suddenly announced that he was leaving her to go to work for a Muslim man nearby. Surprised, Dinesen asked him if he were unhappy working for her. He told her that all was well, but that he had decided to work for a Christian for three months to study the ways of Christians, then work for a Muslim for three months to study the ways of Muslims. After experiencing both, he was going to decide whether to be a Christian or a Muslim.

What about that? What would he choose if he lived among us and saw, when we thought he wasn't looking, what we did and how we acted and how we treated others at home, at school, in the neighborhood, and in the workplace? I wonder. I wonder if, as a result of what he observed, he would turn into a Pontius Pilate or a Sergeant Schultz. What do you think?

Feasts & Celebrations

A Light of Revelation

Luke 2:22–40

This is a powerful gospel that we just heard because it is not just the story of Joseph and Mary and Anna and Simeon. It is the life story of every man and every woman.

Let's consider the four main figures in this story. First there are the parents, Mary and Joseph, people of such moderate means that they had to bring a lesser offering to the Temple for the dedication of their son. They are like all other parents who bring their child to church to be baptized.

When we have baptisms during Mass, I ask the parents holding their newly baptized baby to tell the congregation what they wish for their child. They always wish, as they should, happiness, health, a long life, and that the baby would grow up to be a good person. But poignantly, they also express their fears. They say things like they hope that their child would be safe from harm; that he our she would not get into drugs or violence or casual sex or be corrupted by what they see on TV or by the materialism that could shrink their souls. They hope that their child would not break their hearts or ever have to go to war. In short, they are just like Mary and Joseph, dedicating their child to God and wishing the best for their child. Yet they are aware—very aware—of the possibility that, because of their child, a sword might pierce their hearts as well.

Because of this, it's a good day to pray for all parents who have felt that sword.

Next, there is Anna, who is eighty-four years old! She has

seen it all, including the death of her husband and perhaps even of one or more of her children. She lived in a time when her nation was occupied by Roman soldiers. Political corruption was rampant and routine, led by rulers who would come and go after bleeding their people. There was graft, unjust taxation that fell heavily on the poor, embezzlement, payoffs, suppression and, worst of all, greedy priests ruling the Temple.

In Anna's time, some, like the Zealots, became secret assassins of the Romans, spawning crime in the streets. Others, like the Essenes, found the Temple and the priests so corrupt they took off and founded their own community by the Dead Sea. The Sadducees, who controlled the Temple and sold their souls to the Romans, were the aristocratic corporate leaders of the time. The Pharisees, pious men, concocted rigid burdens and laid them on the backs of the people while they, as Mary and Joseph's child would acidly say when he grew up, lifted not one finger themselves.

And yet, there was Anna. Anna the faithful. Anna the loyal. Anna the holy who fasted and prayed. Today is the day to think of and thank God for the Annas of this world: those who are hurt by corporate corruption, the trampling of all decent values, the sexual abuse of minors by the clergy. They see it all, they feel it deeply, but they remain faithful. They do not disassociate from the public arena but try to make it better. They do not flee the Church but stay in the Temple day and night, working and praying for purification and renewal. They are our hope, our anchor, our faithful ones. Let's hear it for the Annas of the world.

Finally, there is old Simeon. He is a man on a mission, always looking, always searching, always living on the slim hope that he would not die until somehow, sometime, some way, he would see the face of the Lord and know that all his doubts and fears were groundless. Simeon is the searcher, the one who wants to believe but cannot, whose doubts about God, Jesus, the Church gnaw at him or her. Simeon is the one who is perplexed; he is the griever, the senior citizen facing death and wondering if he or she will see the face of the Lord soon. He is the parent who has lost a child, either bodily or spiritually, and wonders at God's absence; the friend at the bedside of a young AIDS victim who curses God; the soul weighted down with depression; a wife hoping for the recovery of her husband.

That is why Simeon is so compelling. Throughout his life the poor man struggled, doubted, searched, prayed, pleaded, and begged for some sign of God's presence, a sign that God really did care, that behind all of the senseless suffering and pain in the world, there was a larger purpose. He did not want to die anymore than we do before he saw some sign, some hope, some palatable love, some glimpse of the divine face. The message of the gospel is that he finally received a sign, and when he did, he sent up his heartfelt song: "Master, now you are dismissing your servant in peace, according to your word; for my eyes have seen your salvation...." Luke hints that all of us Simeons will someday sing that song.

I love this gospel. It's colorful, and it's a great story. I love it because it's your story, and it's my story. But more than that, it is the word of God, and it gives hope to us all: to parents who inevitably will feel the sword one way or another; to ordinary people, married or single, who are oppressed and dejected by so much that is evil in the world; to all Simeons who wonder where God is in the tragedies and unfairness of life. To all of these peoples comes this word of the Lord.

God will write straight with crooked lines. God will have the last word, not we humans. God will reward faithfulness. Most of all, God will honor his promises: those who stay true to his love will look into the face of the Lord one day. We will sing again. Our life will supply the melody; the gospel has already supplied the words: "Master, now you are dismissing your servant in peace, according to your word; for my eyes have seen your salvation, which you have prepared in the presence of all peoples, a light for revelation to the Gentiles and for glory to your people Israel."

We're All Connected

John 6:51–58

This past Monday was Memorial Day, and this Sunday is the feast of the Body and Blood of Christ, also known as Corpus Christi. One celebrates the deeds of the dead, and the other celebrates unity of all the baptized in one Body of Christ. I would like to join the two concepts together.

Let me start off with some unpleasant facts: soldiers left home, lived in barracks, ate military food, suffered hardships in the jungles and deserts, were wounded, and sometimes died far from home. Because they did all this, we are free. What they did affects us all. In a kind of spiritual joining, through some kind of deep connection, the soldier dying on the battlefields of Gettysburg or in the deserts of Saudi Arabia has touched our lives. There's no doubt about it: there is a synergy, a deep action and reaction, that binds the human race.

This common experience contradicts the popular philosophy that we are independent, that we live in a world where each person is a separate atom and a solitary individual, that we are free-floating organisms, a bundle of selfish genes, that we are unrelated and unconnected to others. In such a scenario, pain becomes utterly without meaning and utterly ridiculous. But we don't believe that for a moment. In fact, in the religious terms of today's feast, we are the Body of Christ. We are members of the same body, interconnected by baptism, joined by grace, united by a common Spirit. What we do or fail to do affects others: our love, our rejection, our prayer, our suffering, our pain.

Suffering and pain are hated and feared by modern society. But if you are connected, united, part of the very Body of Christ, then suffering and pain become powerful agents of grace. Nobody wants to experience them, but when they come, they are spiritual barter and spiritual power. That's why, in the old days, we did something else with pain and suffering. If you promise not to laugh, I'll tell you what it is: we could offer it up for the souls in purgatory, or anyone else for that matter. Modern folk find this a quaint thought. It provokes ridicule and smiles. Offering up sufferings for others boggles the modern, individualistic mind.

But Christian truth is different. Simply put, it is this: we are the body of Christ, and we are all connected. Christian witness says that we are in physical, psychic, and spiritual relationship with one another. We can plead for one another, and we can pray for one another. We can offer up acts of courage, endurance, and sufferings for others. Why, we can even die, and somehow in the great cycle of life and love, it can benefit others.

It is not just that Sidney Carlton took the place of his friend on the gallows in Dickens' book *A Tale of Two Cities*. It's not just that St. Maximilian Kolbe took the place of a prisoner in a concentration camp and died in his stead. It's not just that innumerable United States' soldiers in World War I and II, and in the Korean and Vietnam wars, and in all the other wars, died so that we might be free. What's important for us to remember today is that we human beings can do things that affect others because we are spiritually joined. Because we are spiritually united, we can direct our energies and our prayers and our sufferings and deaths.

If you have asthma, for example, is it absurd to offer up your discomfort for those who are suffocating in inner city tenements on a hot summer's day? Lying on your hospital bed, is it silly to offer your pain for those who are languishing in nursing homes? When you are hungry, is it ridiculous to offer up your hunger for those who daily go to sleep without anything to eat? Is it outrageous for you to offer up your migraine headache, your pain, your cancer, your sickness, for hardened sinners? And for those you love? And for those you hate? A society that sells drugs, face lifts, and pills for every occasion says, "Yes, it is absurd. Suffering has no meaning. It has no redemptive value." But we Catholics say it does. By the grace of God, suffering can be redemptive. In an unknown way, we can gain graces for countless others, for we are the Body of Christ.

Let me put what I'm saying in the form of a story. After the usual Sunday evening hymns, the church's pastor slowly stood up, walked over to the pulpit, and before he gave his sermon, briefly introduced a guest minister who was in the service that evening. The pastor told the congregation that the guest minister was one of his dearest childhood friends, and he wanted him to have a few moments to greet the church and share whatever he felt would be appropriate for the service.

With that, an elderly man stepped up to the pulpit and began to speak. "Once upon a time, a father, his son, and a friend of his son were sailing off the Pacific coast," he began, "when a fast approaching storm blocked any attempt to get back to the shore. The waves were so high that, even though the father was an experienced sailor, he could not keep the boat upright, and the three were swept into the ocean as the boat capsized."

The old man hesitated for a moment, making eye contact with two teenagers who were, for the first time since the service began, looking somewhat interested in his story. The minister continued: "Grabbing a rescue line, the father had to make the most excruciating decision of his life: to which boy he would throw the other end of the lifeline? He only had seconds to make the decision. The father knew that his son was a believer in Jesus, a good Christian; he also knew that his son's friend was not and was living a sinful life.

"The agony of his decision could not be matched by the torrent of waves. Finally, as the father yelled out, 'I love you, son!' he threw out the lifeline to his son's friend. By the time the father had pulled the friend back to the capsized boat, his son had disappeared beneath the raging swells into the black of night. His body was never recovered."

By this time, the two teenagers were sitting up straight in the pew, anxiously waiting for the next words to come out of the old minister's mouth. "The father," he continued, "knew his son would step into eternity with Jesus, but he could not bear the thought of his son's friend stepping into an eternity without Jesus. Therefore, he sacrificed his son to save the son's friend." The aged minister then paused and said with fervor, "How great is the love of God that he should do the same for us. Our heavenly Father sacrificed his only begotten son that we could be saved. I urge you to accept his offer to rescue you and take a hold of the lifeline he is throwing out to you in this service."

With that, the old man turned and sat back down in his chair as silence filled the room. Well, within minutes after the service ended, the two teenagers were at the old man's side. "That was a nice story," politely stated one of the boys, "but I don't think it was very realistic for a father to give up his only son's life in hopes that the other boy would become a Christian."

"Well, you've got a point there," the old man replied, glancing down at his worn Bible. As a soft smile broadened his narrow face, he looked up at the boys and said, "It sure isn't very realistic, is it? But standing here today to tell you that story gives me a glimpse of what it must have been like for God to give up his son for me. You see, I was that father, and your pastor over there—he is my son's friend."

Our Founding Fathers

Matthew 16:13–19

Firmum est cor meum—"my heart is firm or faithful"—are the words on the seal of the North American College, the American seminary in Rome. It is a fitting motto for us to remember on the Church's celebration of Founders Day.

Peter and Paul—one called by the Sea of Galilee and the other on the road to Damascus; one the blue-collar fisherman and the other a learned scholar—are founding apostles of the Church. We celebrate them as any country or corporation or organization celebrates the people whose genius gave the original vision and supplied the witness and hard work to make a lasting contribution. We link them together because the two of them singlehandedly cemented the foundation of the Church and literally bet their lives on its future.

Here are some facts. We know for sure that Peter and Paul did not establish the church in Rome: it was already there when they arrived, founded by one of the other apostles or disciples of Jesus. But we also know for sure that Peter and Paul went to Rome to take their message to the center of civilization. They both died there, the two preeminent apostles of the Church, one crucified upside down and the other beheaded. They gave their lives for the One who gave his life for them.

Paul was buried beneath the church we know today as St. Paul's, outside the walls of the city. Peter, of course, is buried under St. Peter's Basilica. We know this because, for centuries, architects wondered why the first church was built on such an inhospitable spot of land, that is, a place which required tons of fill dirt to level out the ground, even though there was already level ground not too far away. The only logical reason was that, from the very beginning, this place must have been special.

Indeed, over the past century, archaeological investigations have uncovered a cemetery used during the reign of the emperor Diocletian. In the Christian section, archaeologists found a box of bones which, according to the graffiti on the walls, turned out to be Peter's. This box was buried, with mathematical accuracy, layers and layers down, directly beneath the high altar of St. Peter's. So now we know why they built the church in such an awkward place. It was ground hallowed by the presence of Peter's grave.

What we still don't know, however, is when all this happened, when Peter and Paul gave their lives for Jesus. Certainly, it was not on the same day. So, as usual, the early Christians were inventive. They solved that mystery by taking advantage of what was already there, namely a secular feast day. They chose June 29 to mark the deaths of Peter and Paul because this was already being celebrated as the day Rome was founded by Romulus. The message inherent in this choice was that if Romulus had founded an old empire, Peter and Paul laid the foundation for a new one: the Christian Church. So that's what we're celebrating today: the founding of the city of Rome and the founders of the spiritual Rome.

There are other things that we know about Peter and Paul. They were both flawed men whose names were changed, something that was highly significant in those days. One was weak— "Depart from me for I am a sinful man, O Lord"—and the other a hothead: "I persecuted the church of Christ." But Simon was summoned to go beyond his weakness and become Peter, a rock on which the church would rest. Saul was summoned to go beyond his fervor as a persecutor of the new movement, to become Paul, apostle to the gentiles, a promoter of the new movement.

They are unlikely candidates for founding fathers, but maybe G. K. Chesterton had it right when he wrote:

All the empires and the kingdoms have failed because of this inherent and continual weakness, that they were founded by strong men and upon strong men. But this one thing, the historical Christian Church, was founded on a weak man and for that reason it is indestructible. For no chain is stronger than its weakest link.

So we remember Peter and Paul. We remember them for the same reason anyone celebrates a Founders Day: to look back and ask, can we recapture the original genius and insights of the founders? Can we regain and renew the vision that urged them on and made them tick?

Consider this: the full title of Prince Charles, the future king of Great Britain, is his Royal Highness Prince Charles Philip Arthur George, Prince of Wales and Earl of Chester, Duke of Cornwall and Duke of Rotheasy, Earl of Carrick, Baron of Renfrow, Lord of the Isles and Great Steward of Scotland. When Jesus was crucified, his title was scratched on a piece of simple wood and attached to the cross: Jesus of Nazareth, the King of the Jews. And when Peter and Paul were martyred in Rome, their titles were simply "apostles." The grander titles would come later to the Church: Your Holiness, Supreme Pontiff, Your Eminence, Most Reverend, Your Grace, My Lord—or in French, Mon Signore, which we use as "Monsignor"—and the rest.

You catch the difference in this comparison. Before he had a title, Peter was walking along the street when, as you may recall, a lame man begged alms from him. Peter famously replied, "Silver and gold I have none, but what I do have I can give: in the name of Jesus Christ, rise up and walk." And the man did.

Centuries later, a poor monk traveled to Rome to speak with Julius II, who showed him the vast riches and priceless treasures of the Church. The amazed monk saw room after room filled with art, sculpture, jewels, and precious metals. The proud pope said to the monk, "You see, my friend, the successor of Peter does not have to say, 'Silver and gold I have none.'" "Yes, Holy Father," replied the monk. "But by the same token, he can no longer say, 'In the name of Jesus Christ, rise up and walk.'"

That's the kind of a story that makes us ask, "Have we lost something along the way?"

What was it that made Peter and Paul tick?

Jesus.

How can we regain their vision?

Jesus.

Peter put it this way: "Lord, to whom shall we go? We have come to believe that you have the words of eternal life."

Paul put it this way: "It is no longer I that live, but Christ lives in me," and "I am determined to know nothing else but Jesus Christ and him crucified."

The feast day of our spiritual Founding Fathers reminds us that if we as the Church have fallen on hard times, could it be because Jesus is no longer the center of our lives—as he was for Peter and Paul? It's a thought, not just for today, but for this time, this place, this heart of yours and mine.

Father's Day

Back when he hosted *The Tonight Show*, Johnny Carson told his audience that one day, his son gave him a paper that read, "To the man who has inspired me with his fatherly wisdom."

Carson said, "Son, I didn't know you felt that way about me."

His son said, "I don't. Can you fax this to Bill Cosby?"

Well, today is Father's Day, and we usually spend it praising Dad. On your behalf, preachers like myself customarily extol him as well. The message is usually from us to him. Today, if you will bear with me, I want to do something different, precisely the opposite. Much to Dad's chagrin, I want to deliver a message from *him* to *us*, a message he may find difficult to give himself. To make this easier on you and me and Dad, I want to deliver this message through the medium of a son's story, a true one. So just relax, and let this story from Ed Nickum, which is actually every dad's story, convey the message to you.

My father lived a hard-working, middle-class life. He had served his country during World War II and held tight to the moral values he gained through the struggles of that era. In all the years of my youth, I knew of only two days of work that Dad missed. His honorable work ethic and quiet, solid manner also gave rise to one of his flaws—my father's inability to express his feelings or to speak aloud about the love he felt for his family. Yet there was one exception to this rule that I will never forget.

One Sunday, my sister, one of my brothers, and my wife and I had gathered at my parents' house for dinner. During the normal chatter, I noticed that my father slurred his words now and then when he spoke. No one mentioned it during dinner, but I felt compelled to discuss it with my mother afterward, as we sipped coffee alone together in the kitchen.

"He says his dentures don't fit anymore," Mom explained. "I've been bugging him for weeks to make an appointment with the dentist, but he keeps putting it off."

"The problem isn't his teeth, Mom. I don't know what's wrong, but he needs to see his doctor, not his dentist. I know he hates to go to the doctor, and I'll help drag him if we have to. I'm really worried."

Drawing on the lessons learned from her many years of marriage to a stubborn man, my mother devised a plan to deliver him to the doctor's office without a struggle. She made an appointment with the dentist, and then called the doctor to explain the situation. The doctor, well aware of the difficulty in getting my father to keep an appointment, went along with the plan. Waiving the normal rules for a specific appointment time, he agreed to see my father immediately after his dental appointment. The dentist, also clued into the conspiracy, pretended to adjust my father's dentures and then sent him on his way. Mom took the "scenic route" home, and before he suspected a thing, Dad found himself in the parking lot of the medical complex. After the standard protest, he quietly followed my mother into the doctor's office. She phoned me two days later.

"I'd like you to come over this evening. We need to talk," she said. I rushed over after work. My mother motioned me into the kitchen. She spoke softly so my father could not hear. "They found a brain tumor," she said. "It's too large at this point to operate. They're going to try to shrink it with radiation and chemotherapy; maybe they can do something then." She stopped to wipe tears from her eyes.

My father soon began to undergo a barrage of treatments. One of the side effects was the loss of almost all of his thick black hair. One of the lighter moments we experienced during this ordeal was when my wife Michele gave birth to our first child, and we all laughed to discover what had happened to Dad's hair: Chelsey arrived in the world wearing it.

My father's condition worsened, and the doctors finally

informed us that his condition was terminal. During one of his prolonged stays in the hospital, we brought Chelsey with us when we visited him. By this time his speech had deteriorated to the point where interpreting the words he tried to form was virtually impossible. Lying in bed, my father's head propped up on pillows, he tried to communicate with me through grunts and hand gestures. I finally figured out that he wanted me to set Chelsey on his stomach, so he could make faces at her. With my father's hands wrapped around her tiny waist, Chelsey sat on her grandpa, and they jabbered nonsense talk back and forth. Chelsey's vocabulary was restricted by her youth, my father's by the horrible disease that was stealing a larger part of his brain with each passing day.

Dad remained in control of his laughter, however, if not his speech. And how he laughed that day. He mumbled and cooed to Chelsey; she returned the volley with a stream of gurgles and slobbery consonants. Then they'd both erupt into deep belly laughs. The bond that grew between grandfather and granddaughter never required a formal language. Dad discovered an ally who fell in love with him completely and unconditionally. Chelsey possessed the child's knack of knowing a grandfather's loving touch when she felt it. After Dad escaped the hospital for the familiar and comfortable surroundings of his own home, the Grandpa/Chelsey comedy routine became a regular part of our visits. Both participants found it hilarious. They laughed every time they played the game, each trying to out-silly the other.

Finally, on a visit to my parents' home during what we all knew were my father's last days, my mother took Chelsey from my arms and announced, "Your father would like to see you alone for a minute." I entered the bedroom where my father lay on a rented hospital bed. He appeared even weaker than the day before. "How are you feeling, Dad?" I asked. "Mom said you wanted to see me. Can I do anything for you?" He tried to speak, but I couldn't make out a word. "I'm sorry, but I can't understand you," I said. "You want your pad and pen?"

Ignoring my suggestion for his pad and pen, he slowly and

with great effort pulled himself higher in the bed. Moved by the intensity of his struggle as he again tried and failed to speak, I reached out to hold his hand.

Our eyes met and locked, both of us suddenly forced to face the painful reality that all the years we'd spent together, as I'd grown from a child to a man with a child of my own, had come down to this one last father-and-son moment. Tears glistened in my father's eyes. He shook his head and smiled at me as if to say, "Ain't this just the damnedest thing?" Then Dad took a deep breath and won one final battle with the disease that would soon win the war. He softly spoke three little words with crystal clarity: "I love you."

We don't learn courage from heroes on the evening news. We learn true courage from watching ordinary people rise above hopeless situations, overcoming obstacles they never knew they could. I saw the courage my mother possessed when she chose to fight the battle that would allow her husband to remain at home where he belonged. I gained courage from our friends, neighbors, and relatives as they drew closer, circling wagons of love around until the last days of my father's life. Most of all, I learned about courage from my father, who simply refused to leave this world until he overcame his greatest obstacle: sharing his heart with his son.

Dads don't always openly share their love. On Fathers' day I just wanted to remind you that it's there. Oh, yes, children, it is there.

Notes

Christ the Ever-Green, page 5
The story of Henry Viscardi is from Eric Feidman's *The Power Behind Positive Thinking* (San Francisco: HarperCollins, 1996).

Let Your Light Shine, page 23
The Sandy Koufax and Eli Herring stories appeared in the *Wall Street Journal* in an article written by Ted Roberts and quoted by William Willimon in January 2002.

Zeal for Your House, page 52
As I mentioned in the introduction, you can replace the local references with those of your own. This is the kind of homily that evokes a reaction from a certain segment of the congregation who protest that "you shouldn't be preaching politics from the altar"—which shows how circumscribed our moral and Christian sensitivities are.

Blindness and Sight, page 57
The story of Doctor Komp is from Diane M. Komp, M.D., *A Window into Heaven* (Zondervan, 1992). The William Montague Dyke story is from Kent Crockett's *Making Today Count for Eternity* (Sister, OR: Multnomah Publishers, 2001).

The Clubhouse, page 61
The date of Stephen King's *Family Circle* article is November 1, 2001.

Keeping Faith, page 65
Even over a year later, the clerical sex scandal is alive, and now and then a new report or summary or case surfaces to remind people of the shame. It's never far from the back of their minds, which is why I have included this homily on the Sunday the

gospel talks about Thomas and faith. I have taken the material from my book *Breaking Trust: A Priest Looks at the Scandal of Sexual Abuse* (Mystic, CT: Twenty-Third Publications, 2001). My instincts to give this homily were validated by the round of applause after it. People still carry the scandal around.

He Descended into Hell, page 77
This striking explanation in the first part of the homily I owe entirely to Richard Rolheiser, whose words appeared in the June 2003 issue of *U.S. Catholic*. The story of John XXIII comes from Thomas Cahill's (somewhat distorted) biography of that pope.

Biblical Saints, page 108
The example of Rahab and its development was modified from William Willimon.

Non-Perishable Food, page 111
The story is Judith Black's version of an old tale, "The King's Child," found in *Ready-to-Tell Tales*, edited by David Holt and Bill Mooney (Little Rock, AR: August House Publishers, Inc., 1994). Used by permission.

Learning to Enjoy Holland, page 139
This touching parable is used by permission.

Choosing Compromise or Christ, page 146
I used the Sergeant Schultz story once before in another book. The story about the freedom riders comes from Thomas G. Long in *Whispering the Lyrics* (Lima, OH: CSS Publishing Co., 1995).

Father's Day, page 164
The story, with minor modifications, is from Ed Nickum and is found in *A Cup of Comfort*, edited by Colleen Sel (Avon, MA: Adams Media Corporation, 2001). Used with permission.